Durham Churches

Durham Churches

COMPILED AND ILLUSTRATED
BY
ROBIN WALTON

First published in 2001 by
Pentland Books
1 Hutton Close
South Church
Bishop Auckland
Durham

British Library Cataloguing in Publication Data.
A catalogue record for this book is available
from the British Library.

ISBN 1 85821 912 4

Typeset by George Wishart & Associates, Whitley Bay.
Printed and bound by Antony Rowe Ltd., Chippenham.

To

Margaret

Whose patience and cheerfulness
made this book possible

Why visit such musty old churches?' –
'There are half of them toppling down.' –
'Honestly I couldn't be bothered.' –
'You missed a good film in town.' –
'Good Heavens! how you surprise me;
I credited you with more sense.' –
'It's time you kept up with the present;
Did not dwell so much with 'Past Tense'.'

Do 'they' really wonder why I go?
Are 'they' really curious to know
Why I love these old churches so?

It is not the architecture –
Saxon, Norman, decorated or plain;
Each church holds a beauty
That for me is all the same.
No . . .

It is because I feel so humble
As I kneel in their pews to pray,
And think of the men who first built them –
How they worked for love, not for pay.
Whilst the sketching was done I wandered
Round the churchyards and inside,
And thought of all those who have worshipped,
Who have been baptized, married, and have died.
Chance I gazed at an old stone coffin,
At holes where a door was once barred,
Read stories of hatred and courage
In walls which are blackened and scarred.
Perhaps sat in a misererë,
Traced carvings that Time has worn bare;
Touched the marble faces of warriors
Whose hands now rest, folded in prayer.
Maybe I heard too the music of angels
As a peal of bells rang through the air;
But wherever I was I marvelled
At a love so expressively there.

God's blessing must be with those builders
Whose faith is still shown us today,
In the glorious churches they leave us
Wherein we can worship and pray.
May God bless this book that is written
That e'en when our sojourn is done,
Its pages bear fruit as a witness
That our faith, like the builders', lives on.

Margaret J. Robinson.

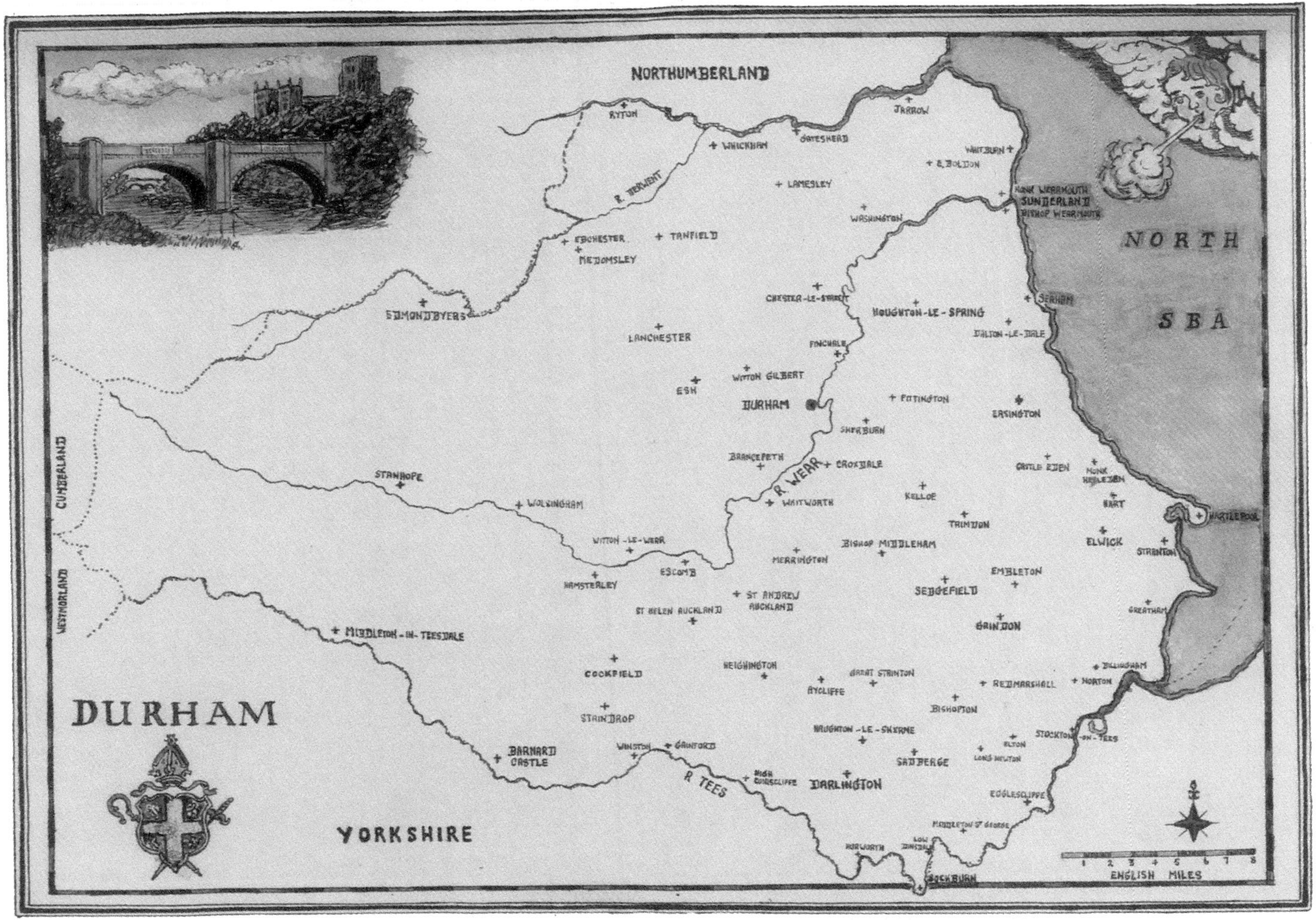
DURHAM
NORTHUMBERLAND
NORTH SEA
YORKSHIRE
CUMBERLAND
WESTMORLAND
ENGLISH MILES
R. WEAR
R. TEES
R. DERWENT
RYTON
WHICKHAM
GATESHEAD
JARROW
WHITBURN
E. BOLDON
LAMESLEY
WASHINGTON
MONK WEARMOUTH
SUNDERLAND
BISHOP WEARMOUTH
EBCHESTER
MEDOMSLEY
TANFIELD
CHESTER-LE-STREET
HOUGHTON-LE-SPRING
SEAHAM
DALTON-LE-DALE
EDMONDBYERS
LANCHESTER
FINCHALE
WITTON GILBERT
ESH
DURHAM
PITTINGTON
EASINGTON
SHERBURN
BRANCEPETH
CROXDALE
CASTLE EDEN
MONK HESLEDEN
HART
HARTLEPOOL
STANHOPE
WOLSINGHAM
WHITWORTH
KELLOE
TRIMDON
ELWICK
STRANTON
WITTON-LE-WEAR
BISHOP MIDDLEHAM
MERRINGTON
ESCOMB
HAMSTERLEY
ST ANDREW AUCKLAND
EMBLETON
SEDGEFIELD
GREATHAM
ST HELEN AUCKLAND
GRINDON
MIDDLETON-IN-TEESDALE
COCKFIELD
HEIGHINGTON
AYCLIFFE
GREAT STAINTON
REDMARSHALL
NORTON
BILLINGHAM
STAINDROP
BISHOPTON
HAUGHTON-LE-SKERNE
STOCKTON-ON-TEES
ELTON
LONG NEWTON
SADBERGE
BARNARD CASTLE
WINSTON
GAINFORD
HIGH CONISCLIFFE
DARLINGTON
EGGLESCLIFFE
MIDDLETON ST GEORGE
HURWORTH
LOW DINSDALE
SOCKBURN

Contents

Introduction

Most of us are interested in churches. Usually people on holiday when visiting a Cathedral city, if they have a few hours to spare will ask 'Can you direct us to the Cathedral?' Then again people going on holiday abroad will make a point of visiting the cathedrals and churches.

The purpose of this book is to introduce people to some of the lesser known churches in Durham. A knowledge of what to look for in a church makes the visit of much greater interest. It lifts us for ever above those who only take a casual glance.

In a work of this size there are bound to be omissions for which I ask to be excused. Firstly, only a small percentage of the county's churches are mentioned, but all of these have a history going back over 200 years. Perhaps some of the interior fittings may now have been moved to another position in the church, in others they may have been removed altogether. There may be many additions since my visit now over 50 years ago.

To turn a corner in the road and there to see before you a little gem of a church is an unforgettable experience. Sometimes a church is surrounded by trees, then it can only be seen on entering the churchyard which in itself can be a veritable source of historical information.

If the reader was to explore all the churches in this book, then they will have covered most of the County of Durham which means the book will have served a double purpose.

To the readers I wish many happy hours of exploration and hope it will give them as much pleasure as it has for me.

Robin Walton

Aycliffe

The village of Aycliffe is supposed to have derived its name from the oak woods which have stood there. Situated on a hill at the west end of the village is the church with its tower about 66 ft high, presenting a landmark which can be seen for many miles.

The church, dedicated to St Andrew, consists of chancel, nave with north and south aisles, south porch and western tower. The earliest parts are the side walls of the nave which are of pre-Conquest date. The rest of the church dates from the 12th and 13th centuries.

The nave was originally an aisle-less one and was much shorter than as at present. The angle quoining of the added portion is clearly visible in the north-east pier of the tower. Towards the end of the 12th century a north aisle was added, the arcade being inserted in the existing wall. This arcade consists of three semicircular arches of two chamfered orders. The arches are surrounded by an indented hood moulding. The eastern pier is cylindrical and the western one octagonal. The south aisle was added in the same way in the 13th century. This arcade consists of three pointed arches, each of two orders. The eastern arch is much higher than the western ones. The piers are cylindrical with moulded capitals. In the east end of the south wall there is a trefoil-headed piscina. The south doorway is original, the arch being of two orders. The porch protecting it was re-erected in 1852.

The tower was built at the same time as the aisle. It is open to the nave and aisles by pointed arches. The one opening into the nave is considerably higher than those opening into the aisles. The last stage of the tower was added in the 15th century and is battlemented. The belfry contains three bells.

The pre-Conquest crosses stand at the west end of the aisles; one bearing representations of two crucifixions, these being of Christ and St Peter.

An effigy of a knight (14th century) lies in the north aisle and close by is a grave-cover of an ecclesiastic of the same date. The font is 12th century. The pews are Jacobean and of excellent character (about 1630).

The chancel arch is pointed and is of two chamfered orders. The responds have moved causing the arch to settle down and consequently take on a much different shape to what it would have been originally. The chancel dates from the 12th century. The east window is modern. In the north wall there are two original round-headed windows. In the south wall is a square-headed priest's doorway with a similar window above it. A very interesting memorial lies on the floor of the chancel; it has been a grave-cover then later an altar stone.

On the south side of the churchyard is a limestone quarry and it is to be feared that blasting operations carried out there will have an effect on the foundations and fabric of the church as stones have been thrown onto the roof at various times.

Barnard Castle

The market town of Barnard Castle is situated in the south-west corner of the county. Perched on a sloping hill are several old stone houses and the ruinous castle, scene of many a siege. Round the foot of the hill flows the turbulent Tees amid its beautiful wooded banks. It comes as a shock to the visitor to find at a short distance from the ancient town a modern building resembling in design the Hotel de Ville at Le Havre. This is Bowes Museum, one of the finest museums in the country.

The church dedicated to St Mary the Virgin dates from the 12th century. It consists of chancel with north and south transepts, nave with north and south aisles, and a north-western tower. The entrance to the church is through a north door in the tower. The tower is entirely modern (1874) but is in the style of the one it replaced. The south doorway is perhaps one of the most interesting features of the church. It is round-headed. The arch is of three orders and each order has its own nook-shafts. The font in the base of the tower dates from about 1480.

The north arcade consists of four bays, the two western bays being original. These are semi-circular and consist of two square plain orders. The two eastern bays were rebuilt in 1870. The south arcade was rebuilt about the end of the 13th century. It consists of five pointed arches, each of two plain chamfered orders. The arches rest on octagonal pillars.

The transepts date from the middle of the 15th century. In the north wall of the north transept there are two recesses intended for, and probably once occupied by, the effigies of benefactors. In one of these recesses lies a badly mutilated effigy of a priest. The other recess contains several sculptured gravestones. In the east wall there is a piscina. The south transept also has a piscina in the south wall.

To enter the chancel, which is much higher than the nave, one has to climb six steps. The chancel arch is perpendicular and is decorated with rudely carved roses. Over the arch on the north side there is a walled-up square-headed doorway. This was probably part of the rood-loft.

The nave clerestory dates from the same time as the south arcade. In the nave there is a north porch which is not in use, its outer door being walled up.

An interesting custom which has been in practice for over 200 years is the distribution every Sunday of loaves of bread to the poor of the parish.

In the churchyard the most interesting memorial is a large altar tomb. It stands near the south wall of the nave at the west end and is very elaborately decorated.

Billingham

The village of Billingham is situated about two and a half miles north-east from Stockton on the Stockton–Sunderland road.

The church, dedicated to St Cuthbert, consists of chancel, nave with north and south aisles, south porch and a western tower.

The chancel is entirely modern and was built in 1937. It has side aisles and contains three altars. In the north wall there is a stone, with the brass removed to a priest.

The tower is Saxon. In the lowest stages there are several single round-headed lights and on the south side there is in the second stage a single round-headed light with imposts. The highest stage has windows on each side of two round-headed lights, separated by a central cylindrical shafts which carry imposts. The space above the lights on the north and south sides is pierced with a star-shaped opening. On the east and west ones the opening is circular. In the base of the tower there is a stone vaulting of early English date.

The arcades which have been inserted in the walls of the early Saxon nave are each of five bays. The south arcade, whose arches are moulded with the dog tooth ornament, is some 30 years later than that of the north arcade. All the arches are pointed. The piers of the north arcade are masses of walled Saxon masonry. The imposts consist of a fillet and a chamfer with a nutmeg ornament on each of the chamfer. The south arcade is of a much elaborate character. Each pier has a central cylinder resting on a square plinth with four slender shafts attached. The chancel arch is also pointed and consists of two chamfered orders. This arch is of the same date as the arcade and the ancient chancel which was destroyed also belongs to that time. The font is of the same date as the south arcade and is decorated with leaf ornaments in the lower part. In the north wall of the nave there is a blocked doorway. At the east end of the north aisle there is an early niche.

The parapet of the clerestory is battlemented and has four grotesque gargoyles. The roof is of oak and dates from the end of the 15th century.

Built into the walls of the porch there are several fragments of medieval grave-covers.

At the west end of the nave, on the wall of the tower, there is a minute clock.

Bishopton

The village of Bishopton is about six miles from Stockton and one mile west of Redmarshall.

The church is dedicated to St Peter and it is on St Peter's day (29th June) that the parish feast is held. The original church was Norman but the present building was almost entirely rebuilt in 1846–7.

The church consists of a nave with north aisle and chancel. At the west end is the tower. The main entrance to the church is here. Parts of the chancel walls are ancient. A 13th century one light window has been inserted north of the chancel arch. Under the east window are two dedication crosses and two medieval grave-covers are built into the walls. At the back of the church are two medieval oak chests and a Norman font.

Near the churchyard gate there is a 1914–18 War Memorial cross and near to that again is an ancient cross, probably the ancient village cross.

In a field at the south end of the village is a large artificial hill, about 40 ft high, called 'Castle Hill.' This mound is first mentioned as being fortified by Roger de Conyers after his banishment by the Usurper Comin, and here he resisted the large army sent against him. The mound is surrounded by other earthworks and is probably of very early British date.

Bishop Middleham

Bishop Middleham is a delightful village situated about two miles from Ferryhill Station. In a field south of the church can be seen grass-covered mounds now all that remain of the castle belonging to the Bishops of Durham. Here died in 1316 Bishop Kellaw whose ancestors came from Kelloe, about 4 miles to the north. There is a popular belief that the village takes its name from Bishop's Middle Home, the other two homes being Auckland Castle and Durham Castle.

The church is dedicated to St Michael and is nearly all of one date, about the 13th century. It consists of nave, chancel, north and south aisles, a north porch and a bell-cot on the west gable. A church is known to have existed here in 1146.

The nave is divided from the aisles by arcades of four pointed arches. The hood mouldings of the arcades end in grotesque heads, some being animals with rings through their mouths. Above the arcade of the south aisle is a clerestory of four windows which are modern except for the openings. In the west end of the nave there is a round-head window, the sill being considerably higher than those of the other windows.

In the east end of the south aisle there is a piscina but no trace is found of one in the north aisle. At the west end of the north aisle there is the font of Frosterley marble which probably dates from the 13th century. The bowl of the old stone font lies on the floor; it was found in use as a cattle trough on a nearby farm. Over the interiors of both south and north doorways there are escutcheons.

In the east wall the window of triplet lancets is modern. On the north wall of the chancel there are memorial tablets, one being to Surtees, the local historian. In the south wall, near the west end, there is a low-side window.

Numerous early grave-covers are built into the walls of the interior of the porch. Over the south door is a sundial, dated 1741. Built into the west gable is a circular stone bearing a cross moline. The bell-cot has been rebuilt from the original stones and contains two bells, one probably dates back to the 14th century, the other is dated 1723. A cardinal cross is on the east gable.

The church was in a ruinous state until restored by the widow of the aforementioned Surtees, writer of *The History of the County Palatine of Durham*. He is buried in the churchyard. The church was again restored in 1906.

The first rector was in 1146. In 1278 it was instituted as a Vicarage by Bishop Robert de Insula and annexed to Finchale Priory, the first record of a vicar being 1310. The registers date from 1559.

In the distance can be seen the neighbouring church of Sedgefield. On the night of our visit we could hear the sound of the bells floating across the meadows as they had done for centuries past.

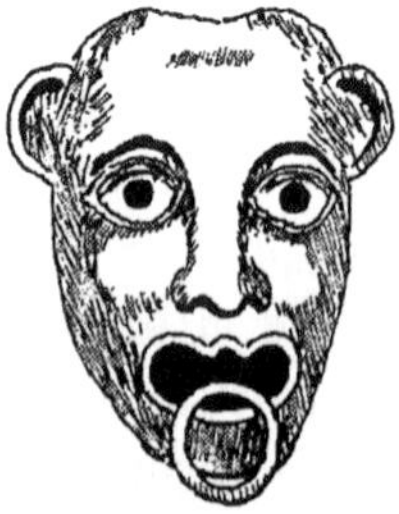

Head in nave.

Bishopwearmouth

The parish of Bishopwearmouth is now swallowed up by Sunderland. The church, dedicated to St Michael, stands at the west end of the High Street. It consists of a chancel, nave with side aisles, north and south transepts, and a western tower.

The church was largely rebuilt in 1934–5 and from the outside the difference in the old and modern stonework is obvious. Previous to this the building was greatly enlarged in 1850 when the transepts were added. The tower was taken down and rebuilt in 1806 and the chancel reduced to its present size.

The oldest remaining parts of the church are the four round massive arches of the tower and parts of the chancel.

The chancel retains its ancient window of five pointed lights under one arch. There are decorated windows in the north and south walls.

In the south transept lies the worn effigy of a knight, Thomas Middleton of Silksworth, who died in 1400. There are several old grave-covers lying alongside this effigy.

The tower contains 8 bells, the heaviest weighing 12 cwts. This bell killed a man while he was muffling it and the lectern is a memorial to that sad incident. Under the tower there is an old font, found during renovations.

The whole church contains some beautiful woodwork, the pews, chancel screen, pulpit and galleries all being made at the famous workshop of Robert Thompson of Kilburn in Yorkshire.

West Boldon

The village of West Boldon is about four miles from Whitburn and the same distance from Sunderland. It is well known as having given its name to the 'Boldon Buke', a survey drawn up in 1183 by Bishop Pudsey. The better known survey of the 'Domesday Book' did not take into account Durham County.

The church is dedicated to St Nicholas. On entering the churchyard one's attention is immediately arrested by the unusual tower and spire. This tower is the only remaining part of the original church, with the exception of the chancel arch, and dates from 1220. The spire rises from the external face of the tower walls without either a set-off or parapet. From the cardinal sides of the octagon, dormers project; these rise from the base of the spire and contain single lancets. A spire of this period is very rare.

About the middle of the 13th century the arcades and aisles were erected. The south porch, although the walls and the pitch of the roof have been lowered, also dates from this time.

The tower arch is a plain one of three chamfered orders, the capitals being richly moulded. The aisles are divided from the nave with arcades of three pointed arches of two chamfered orders. The piers with their capitals and bases are octagonal. The south aisle had a chantry. In the south wall there is a trefoil-headed piscina with grooves for a shelf. Where the altar stood can be seen a string of dog-tooth moulding which has been restored. In the south wall there are two recesses. In the east one lies the sepulchral effigy of a priest. The west one, the older recess of the two, is empty but was intended for the effigy of the founder of the chantry.

The chancel probably dates from the 13th century. It contains a sedilia and a double piscina. Within the altar rails in a modern recess on the north side lies the effigy of another priest which is of the same date as that in the south aisle. There are two Jacobean chairs in the sanctuary. Some of the choir stalls are also Jacobean.

The windows of the church are modern with the exception of those in the tower. The church contains numerous painted figures which were brought from France and Italy by a former vicar.

In the churchyard the visitor finds he is midway between the Wear and Tyne. The jibs of the cranes in the shipyards along each river, point like skeleton fingers to the sky on the northern and southern horizons.

Brancepeth

The village of Brancepeth is four and a half miles west of Durham. It is a truly rural village with its castle and church surrounded by lovely parkland. The castle, onetime home of the Nevilles and now much restored, was the headquarters of the DLI, the County Regiment.

The church of St Brandon is an interesting one. It is built in the cruciform plan, the oldest parts being the tower and the two western bays of the nave arcades.

The nave consists of north and south aisles. The arcades of these aisles consist of pointed arches of two plain chamfered orders resting on octagonal piers with octagonal capitals and bosses. These arches, with the exceptions of the eastern bays, date from the 13th century. The two eastern bays of each aisle are 14th century. The clerestory is divided by buttresses into six bays with a three light window in each and dates from the 14th century. The nave roof is a good example of this period. The principals rest on a fine corbel table.

The transepts were built in the 14th century. The south transept has two windows of decorated date each having three lights. The north transept also contains two windows, the one in the north wall having been restored. The east one is a copy of the original.

The chancel arch is 13th century but its present position is not its original one. The chancel has a chapel on its south side and a vestry on its north; all date from the 14th century. The door into the vestry is original. In the south wall of the vestry is a hagioscope looking into the chancel, and in the west wall a stone basin with a drain leading into the churchyard. The chapel opens to the chancel by a semi-circular arch of one order and has a hagioscope in the north wall and a piscina in the south. In this chapel there is also a beautiful 14th century chest and a black wooden helmet, used in bygone days at funerals of important people, fixed to the wall. There are two other hagioscopes, one each side of the chancel arch. The east window is of five lights the tracery being the transition from the Decorated to the Perpendicular style. There is a piscina in the south wall and on the floor on the north side a stone effigy of a cross-legged knight, probably Robert Neville slain at Berwick, 1319. On the south side there are effigies of Ralph Neville, who died 1484, and one of his two wives. Both are carved in wood and wear collars of Yorkist roses. All the choir stalls have misericords carved with foliage and, together with the chancel screen, date from the 17th century. Over the chancel arch there are two remarkable pieces of screen work, the lower one consisting of carved panels of intricate and delicate tracery, and the upper one bearing carved bosses showing the instruments used during the Crucifixion of Our Lord.

The tower is in three stages and opens to the nave with a pointed arch of two chamfered orders. Beneath the parapet is a corbel table, some of the corbels being carved. In the base of the tower is an altar tomb to Ralph Neville, died 1523, which stood originally in the chapel on the south side of the chancel.

The north porch is 17th century. There is a sanctus bell-cot on the east gable of the nave and built into the churchyard wall are medieval grave-stones forming a stile.

St Brandon's was seriously damaged by fire 16th September 1998.

Castle Eden

Castle Eden is about three miles from Blackhall and is one of the most beautiful places in the Durham coalfield. The village itself consists of two small rows of whitewashed houses and a little to the north of these close by the entrance to Castle Eden Castle and the famed Castle Eden Dene, stands the church.

The church is dedicated to St James and was built in 1764 on the site of a much earlier one. It was enlarged in 1896 when the two aisles were added. The interior is very clean and neatly decorated. Perhaps the most interesting features are the beautiful stained glass windows.

There is a much worn effigy of a priest of the 13th century within the altar rails, and on the east wall of the organ chamber are two decorated grave-covers. The font has an oval basin of white marble and is 17th century.

In the churchyard are two octagonal stones said to be from one of the city gates of Durham. At the east end of the churchyard lie buried most of the Burdon family, the last owners of Castle Eden Castle.

Chester-le-Street

Chester-le-Street is six miles north of Durham and, as its name indicates, is built on the site of a Roman station. At various times several remains of the Roman occupation have been found here and some of these finds are now preserved in the church.

The church, dedicated to St Mary and St Cuthbert, has a very long history. In AD 882 the monks from Lindisfarne built themselves a wooden church to house the coffin of St Cuthbert whose body they had carried with them for seven years, and here it lay for 113 years. During this time the church became the county's cathedral and had nine bishops, the last of whom, Aldhune, moved the see to Durham in AD 995.

The present building dates from the beginning of the 13th century and consists of nave with side aisles, chancel and a western tower with spire. The oldest parts of the church are the north and south walls of the chancel.

The nave is separated from the aisles by 13th century arcades of pointed arches. These arcades at first only had three bays but later two were added to each side at the west end. The most interesting feature of the church is the 'Aisle of tombs', a long line of 14 effigies which occupy the full length of the north aisle. These are of the Lumley family and cover a period from 1100–1550. With the exception of three, all were carved in the 16th century. At the east end of this aisle there is a gallery called the Lambton pew which was erected in 1829. Beneath this in the crypt lies Master Lambton who died a few weeks after Sir Thomas Lawrence painted his portrait, now so well known as 'The Red Boy'.

Anchorage window.

In the south aisle there is a trefoil-headed piscina at the east end, and a square aumbry in the south wall. In the south wall of the nave at the west end there is an Early English window, its two lights being trefoilated and the opening above them quatrefoilated.

At the west end of the north aisle there is an anchorage and inserted in the wall of the upper room is a hagioscope which would look onto the altar in the south aisle. A curious window carved from a single piece of stone is in the outer west wall of the anchorage which faces the street.

The lofty chancel arch is of the same date as the nave arcades. In the chancel in the south wall there are 13th century sedilia with trefoil-headed arches. Three early 13th century windows which illustrate the development of window tracery, consist of lancets with an arch above them, the wall space above the lancets and below the arch being pierced, in one case by a circle, in another by a quatrefoil and in the third by a lozenge shaped opening. On the same wall is a brass to Alice Lambton who died in 1434. On the north wall three large modern paintings portray the early history of Chester-le-Street.

At the west end of the church there is a large 15th century font and close by several fragments of Saxon crosses and the 13th century effigy of a priest. In the base of the tower are several relics from the Roman station, the most interesting being the bust of an Emperor, the only known example to be found in England.

The lower part of the tower is square and Early English, the upper part being octagonal and, with the spire, of Perpendicular date, about 1400. The spire rises to a height of 156 ft, making a fine landmark.

Cockfield

The village of Cockfield is situated six miles south-west from Bishop Auckland. It stands on the famed Cockfield Fell, a windswept common noted for flocks of geese which were bred there.

The church is dedicated to St Mary and consists of chancel, nave with a north aisle and a south porch. The church was greatly enlarged and restored in 1911, the north aisle dating from this time. The oldest parts of the church are the chancel and part of the nave, these dating from the 13th century.

The chancel has a triplet of lancets in its east wall; the heads of these windows are modern. A priest's door and a low-side window in the south wall are now walled up. There is also a piscina and aumbry in this wall. Within the altar rails there are grave-covers to a priest and a knight. The knight's cover has a raised cross and shield, and the name, Roger Vavasour, is inscribed on the stone. Close by lies the effigy of a girl which is 3'8" long and of the 14th century.

The nave is panelled along the lower part of the walls with the wood of the old box pews. In the south wall, nearly hidden by the pulpit, there is a piscina. The chancel screen which divides the nave from the chancel is a 1914–18 memorial to a local soldier. The aisle, which was built in 1911, has a piscina in the north wall which was originally in the north wall of the nave. Built into the walls there are several ancient grave-covers. The font which stands at the west end of the aisle is a large octagonal basin resting on a square pillar.

High Coniscliffe

The village of High Coniscliffe is about 4 miles west of Darlington. The church, with the vicarage and the churchyard, is perched on the edge of a limestone cliff and from the river side presents a very striking and imposing sight.

Dedicated to St Edwin, the church consists of a western tower with a spire attached, north porch, chancel and nave with a north aisle. The chancel has a vestry on the north side with an upper priest's apartment. The church was restored in 1844, the roof of the nave being rebuilt. The north wall of the nave and the east window also date from this time.

The north doorway is ancient. It has round Norman arches of two orders, both ornamented with beak-heads. Also Norman are the western gable of the nave and the western part of the south wall; a break in this wall shows the point of junction of the earlier and later work. The rest of the church belongs to the 13th century except for the spire which was added in the 14th century.

The nave is separated from the aisle by four cylindrical pillars, each little more than 6 ft high, supporting pointed arches. In the west wall is a square-headed doorway being the entrance to the basement of the tower. The nave and chancel are of equal height and are divided by a pointed arch of two orders. This arch is highly decorated, the inner order resting on keel-shaped responds which have carved and moulded capitals. The neck of the capitals is carved with conventional foliage.

In the chancel there is only one original window; a lancet in the north wall. The doorway leading into the vestry is round-headed and is also original. The stalls are 15th century the bench-ends having boldly designed Poppy-heads, some of which contain figures of demi-angels.

There are grave-covers in the sanctuary, nave and north aisle. The vestry probably dates from the 15th century and the apartment above it was no doubt the quarters of a chantry priest, as at Houghton-le-Spring.

The clerestory was added in the 14th or 15th centuries but has been restored to such an extent that to give a precise date is not possible. It is unusual in the fact that the windows are over the piers and not over the centre of the arches.

The font is plain, resting on a cylindrical shaft, and is 13th century.

The tower is battlemented and the spire, which is octagonal, was added in the 14th century. On the eastern walls of the tower can been seen the coping of the Early English roof.

Croxdale

This church dedicated to St Bartholomew was formerly a Chapel-of-Ease to St Oswald's, Durham, and is now the property of the Salvins at Croxdale Hall. An exchange of land took place in 1845–6 in which the site of the modern church was given in exchange for this now ruined chapel. The chapel is very pleasantly situated approximately three quarters of a mile from the village of Croxdale and makes a picture worth remembering if visited when the two chestnut trees, which flank the south-east side of the churchyard wall, are bearing their pink candles.

The most striking feature in the churchyard is the old wooden cross purported to have been erected to keep away the evil spirits. These are supposed to have lurked in the dell 'so deep and narrow that the sun's rays are excluded almost throughout the year.' The village no doubt derives its name from this (Croix-dale).

There is no register of burials and there are no grave stones recording the same prior to the chapel becoming privately owned.

The chapel consists of nave and chancel with bell-cot on the west gable. The south doorway is early Norman. On the tympanum is a well weathered sculpture appearing to have represented the branches of a tree projecting from a central horizontal stem terminating with a human. The lintel bears a line of square star ornament. The iron bands of the hinges on the door are original.

The chancel has a flat roof and the nave a high pitched one which is pantiled.

The chancel arch is late Transitional, semicircular and of two plain chamfered orders. A door in the north wall of the chancel is walled in. On the floor are two incised crosses. The three plagues on the north wall are erected to the members of the Salvin family.

The nave walls have been panelled half way up but this is in a very decayed state. On the floor are two bells of the long-waisted shape; one is broken and uninscribed, the other is dated 1607. The font which lies broken in three pieces is inscribed 1147.

The east window is a beautiful three light 14th century window with flowing tracery of an excellent design. There are lancet windows in the north and west walls of the nave. The remaining windows are sash ones of modern date.

The key to the churchyard and church is kept at nearby Croxdale Hall.

Dalton-le-Dale

The little village of Dalton-le-Dale is about six miles south of Sunderland on the coast road from there to Stockton. A pleasant walk can be taken to the village through the dene from Seaham Harbour.

The church, dedicated to St Andrew, is a plain structure consisting of a chancel, nave and south porch with a bell-cot on the west gable. Most of the building is Early English with the exception of the south porch and a Norman doorway in the north wall of the nave. The south porch, which shelters a 13th century doorway was added about 1450. This doorway has a pointed arch of two orders, the jambs originally having nook shafts which have now disappeared. The Norman doorway dates from about 1150, its round-headed arch having a peculiar kind of chevron moulding.

A recess in the north wall contains the badly mutilated effigy of a 15th century woman. Nearby is a low-side window which has a pointed trefoil head. Along the north wall is one of the most remarkable objects to be found in a Durham county church, a row of raised Roman numerals from seven to one forming part of a sundial. Originally the sun's rays passed through a slit in the roof above the middle window in the south wall to record the hours from 7 a.m. to 1 p.m. The font is very similar to that in Seaham church. Two brackets on the south wall of the nave are like those in the chancel. There is a benitura by the left side of the south door.

The chancel is not now separated from the nave by an arch but there has been a Norman arch which was removed in the 19th century. A recess in the north wall of the chancel contains an effigy of a knight believed to be Sir William Bowes who died in 1420. To the east of this there is a plain altar tomb of black marble.

The east window is a triplet of lancets, on each side of which there is a bracket intended for images. The south wall contains two lancet windows and a low-side window similar to that in the nave. In the same wall there is a priest's door visible on the exterior but blocked by the organ in the interior. The north wall has a two light window. The head contains a quatrefoil with pierced cusps.

Outside, above the south porch, just where the ridge of the porch roof meets the nave wall, there is a very early sundial.

The old vicarage lies a little to the north east of the church. The door-head is four centred and an inscription reads 'Thomas Sharp 1670'.

Darlington

That a church existed at Darlington before the Norman Conquest was proved by the discovery during restorations of several portions of pre-Conquest crosses. The present church, dedicated to St Cuthbert, is more like a miniature cathedral. It is built in the cruciform plan and has an ancient vestry on the south side of the chancel.

The nave is divided from the aisles by arcades of four pointed arches on each side. The arches of the eastern bays are richly moulded but the remainder are plain, consisting of three chamfered orders. The first pier on each side is composed of clustered shafts. In the clerestory, close to the tower, there is a single bay of an arcade on each side. The western piers are alternately cylindrical and octagonal and are arranged so that an octagonal pier is opposite a cylindrical one. The clerestory has four obtuse pointed lights on each side. About the middle of the 14th century many alterations took place. The aisles walls were raised and the present windows inserted in the aisles. Previous to this the aisles were vaulted, evidence of which is visible in the springer of one of the vaulting ribs on the first pier from the west. There is a door in the west end of the nave and in the north and south walls. All are originals.

The transepts have two tiers of arcades on the walls. The north transept is plainer than the south but it is of an earlier date. Here for some reason work ceased for a while, during which time the style was changing. The mouldings intended for square abaci rest on round ones and some have the Transitional volute below them and show that the capital has been altered. The south transept is the most enriched part of the church. The tiers of arcades are richly moulded with nail-head ornaments. In this transept there are two piscinas, both trefoil-headed, one in the east wall the other in the south. There is an aumbry beside the latter. In the south-west corner there is a turret which projects into the transept and also into the churchyard. It is square below and octagonal above and contains a newel stairway.

The tower rests on four obtuse pointed arches with moulded orders. The western arch has the nutmeg ornament on the outer moulding on both sides; the east, north and south arches have it only on the inner sides. The highest stage of the tower and spire date from the 14th century. Each side of the tower has an arcade of five arches, the head of each being filled with Decorated tracery. The central arch on each side is a belfry window. The spire is octagonal. During a severe storm in 1750 it was struck by lightning and part of it had to be rebuilt in 1752. The overall height is 180 ft.

The chancel arch is pointed and the whole width is taken up by a rood screen of plain stone. The church is the only one in the county to retain its rood loft. The east wall of the chancel is modern. The reredos is a beautiful piece of mosaic work originally designed for Westminster Abbey. Each side wall has two arcades of pointed arches, one above the other. Each arcade consists of five bays, the arches being moulded. The windows are decorated with nail-head ornament, others with lozenge-shaped panels on the outer member of the arch.

There is a triplet of sedilia of Decorated date in the south wall. The arches are ogee-shaped and trefoiled. In the north wall there is an arched recess of a late date. In each side of the choir stalls are misericords with carved elbows dating from 1430.

The church contains one sepulchral effigy. It is of a lady (13th century); she holds a book in her hand and her head is covered with a veil.

Externally the church is very richly decorated. The west door is pointed and set in a projection with an arch of three richly moulded orders. In the second stage of the west gable there is an arcade of five arches, the second and fourth arches being pierced by lancet lights. In the last stage of this gable there is a triplet of arches the centre one being pierced by a lancet. The north doorway of the nave has been restored and is set in a square projection. The south doorway of the nave was originally covered by a porch. The clerestory has on each side an arcade of twelve arches. The first, fourth, seventh and tenth arches on each side, counting from the east, are pierced by lancets. In the twelfth arch on the south side there is a sun-dial. The parapet is supported by corbel tables. The chancel and transepts are divided into two stages by moulded string courses. Beneath the parapet there are corbel tables. The south transept externally is more enriched than that of the north. On the west side of this transept the window arches have nail-head and dog-tooth mouldings.

The clock on the tower originally played tunes every fourth hour.

Easington

Easington Village is situated on the Sunderland–Stockton road and with its elevated position commands a good view of the coast. The church, dedicated to St Mary the Virgin, is on the highest point and its tower makes a fine observation point on a clear day.

With the exception of the tower the church is Early English. The tower is Norman, the buttresses probably being added in the 13th century. The main entrance to the church is through a doorway in the south wall of the tower. This doorway is a 19th century addition. The tower arch is round-headed and is depressed. The belfry contains three bells, two of which are dated, 1618 and 1664.

The nave has arcades of four pointed arches on each side, resting on piers alternately circular and octagonal, not only from east to west, but also between north and south. Each arch is of two chamfered orders with hood-mouldings on the nave side. The capitals are moulded, some having ribbed upright leaves, a Norman volute survival in Early English architecture. The clerestory has four small lancet windows, one window being above the centre of each bay of the arcades. Such windows are a rarity. The 17th century bench ends of the nave pews have poppy heads.

The aisles contain no original windows excepting the Early English lancets in the west wall on each side. At the east end of the south aisle lies an effigy of a knight in full armour; it is that of Marmaduke Fitz Galfrid, one of the Lords of Horden, who died towards the end of the 13th century. On the shield are three popinjays; these have been incorporated in the new coat of arms for the town at Peterlee. Nearby is a stone coffin, and on the windowsill above there is a 17th century tilting helmet belonging to one of the Conyers of Horden Hall. At the east end of the north aisle lies an effigy of a woman in late 13th century dress. Wife of one of the Fitz Marmadukes, she was an ancestor of Robert de Brus, King of Scotland. The old box pews now act as panelling round the walls of both aisles.

The lofty chancel arch is the full width of the chancel and rests on semi-octagonal corbels. The east window of five lancets is modern and replaces a three-light window. A priest's doorway in the south wall is now blocked. There is a low-side window in the usual position containing modern glass portraying Bernard Gilpin who ministered here from 1556–60.

The vestry has registers dating back to 1571. In a copy of the *Solemn League and Covenant* of 1645 some of the signatures are only marks.

Ebchester

The village of Ebchester lies in the beautiful Derwent valley about three and a half miles from Consett. Here stand the remains of a Roman station. During the years the local builders have drawn on this station for their building materials and several buildings in the village, including the church, contain Roman masonry.

The church, dedicated to St Ebba, consists of a chancel, nave with a vestry on its south side, and a tower at its north-west corner. The building, with the exception of the vestry and the tower, dates from the 11th century.

The main entrance into the church is by a door in the north wall of the tower. A Roman altar stands in a recess in the west wall of the basement of the tower.

The nave has two original windows in the west wall; the other, and much larger window, is modern. Only one of the windows in the side walls is original. On the north wall there are two escutcheons. Over the chancel arch there is another, only half of which is visible, the remainder being hidden by the low ceiling. The chancel arch consists of a single course of voussoirs with plain angles and soffit. It springs from plain imposts chamfered on the lower edge. The projection of the imposts is only across the soffit. The font is the original Norman one.

The chancel has four of its original windows. These are very small and are deeply splayed inside with sills stepped in three grades. The round heads are cut in a single stone. The heads inside were formed by wooden lintels but these have been replaced by stone. There is an aumbry in the east wall which is modern. Underneath the altar is the original altar stone.

The churchyard stands in the south-west corner of the Roman station. In the base of the west gable there is a piece of carved Roman masonry. The lower courses of the north wall of the church consist of squared stones, probably Roman. The double bell-cot was added in the 13th century.

The beauty of the church has been greatly destroyed by the erection of the tower in 1910.

In the churchyard lies buried Robert Smith Surtees, the sporting novelist, who died at Brighton in 1864. The memorial west window portrays a company of kneeling saints; the faces of two of these resemble the widow of Surtees and their eldest son.

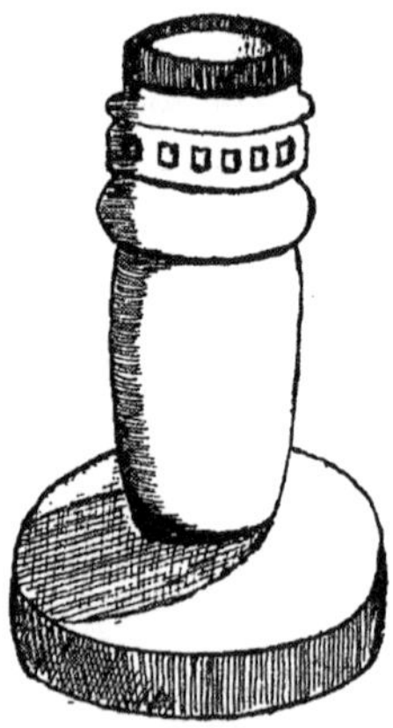

The font.

Edmondbyers

The village of Edmondbyers is a small unpretentious village situated among the hills, about 19 miles due west of Gateshead. It is here we find some of the county's wildest country.

The small church is dedicated to St Edmund and was founded about 1150. It consists of chancel, nave with a south porch, and a bell-cot on the west gable.

We enter the church through the south porch which has the gravestone of a medieval priest built into its west wall. On entering the nave the first thing which meets the eye is an unusual wooden enclosure in the north-west corner. This was made from wood taken from Auckland Castle, Durham Castle, Durham Cathedral and St Mary, Redcliffe, Bristol. The door is from Riding Mill Hall. On the west wall there is a gravestone, supposed to be that of a local witch.

The nave is divided from the chancel by a round arch with a small arch on either side. The chancel has a round-headed piscina and an aumbry. The altarstone is the original one which was found during restorations. The east window is modern.

Close to the church stands the vicarage. The view from the churchyard of the heather clad hills is enchanting.

Egglescliffe

The village of Egglescliffe is on the Durham side of the river Tees, about four miles south-west of Stockton. The houses and cottages cluster round the village green in true English fashion.
The church, dedicated to St Mary, consists of chancel, nave with a chapel on the south side, south porch, and a western tower.

The church dates from Norman times, but the only portions belonging to this period are the north wall of the nave, the jambs of the chancel arch, and the south doorway of the nave.

The chancel is late Perpendicular and, together with the two windows in the south wall and one in the north, dates from the latter half of the 15th century. The east window has five lights. A sedilia and priest's door are in the south wall. The roof of the chancel, the stall work and the screen are all late 17th century. Within the chancel rails are three old chairs; two of Charles II reign and the other Queen Anne.

The chapel known as Pemberton Porch on the south side of the nave was built about the middle of the 14th century. It has two arches which rest on a central octagonal pillar. There are two windows in the south wall and in a recess between them lies the effigy of a man dressed in chain mail. On a desk above this are two chained folio books, Bishop Jewell's *Apology* and the *Eikon Baslike*.

Elton

The name, Elton, means 'Town of Eels', and the village bearing this quaint name lies about three miles from Stockton, on the Stockton to Darlington road.

The church, dedicated to St John, was almost entirely rebuilt in 1841, and consists of nave, chancel and a south porch. There is a bell-cot, containing two small bells, on the west gable.

The nave is divided from the chancel by three small arches. The arches on each side have mouldings of chevron and the centre arch which is Norman is adorned with chevron and beak-head mouldings. All three are filled in with a screen of exquisite workmanship, made in 1907. In the centre arch is a carved wooden figure of Christ on the cross and at each side two figures. The doors are painted with pictures of saints. In the north-east corner of the nave stands a statue of the Virgin Mary and Child.

The inner arch of the south doorway has chevron mouldings. A door in the north wall of the chancel leads into the vestry and has a moulding of nail-head ornament over the arch.

The east window is modern and a memorial, it depicts the Crucifixion and the Resurrection.

Within the altar rails lies a recumbent effigy, thought to represent Robert Gower, who died in 1315. The head rests on a cushion, the face is uncovered, the hands are clasped on the breast, the legs which are crossed have spurs attached at the heels and the feet rest on a lion.

In the churchyard rest the remains of one Mary Benton, who is stated to have been 116 years of age when she died in 1853. There appear to be no burials on the north side.

When the chancel was rebuilt in the 15th century the nave was greatly altered, a doorway (now blocked) and two windows being inserted in the north wall. The oak box pews and the pulpit with its sounding-board are 18th century. The font at the west end is Early English but its cover is late 17th century.

The tower is 15th century and is embattled with corner pinnacles. It also has an embattled projection on the south to the height of the belfry. In the west wall at the lowest stage there is an inserted window of Perpendicular character. It is filled with stained glass and depicts Christ wearing a hat, which is quite unusual. One of the bells is early 15th century.

Elwick

The picturesque village of Elwick consisting of one long street is four miles from Hartlepool. The church stands at the west end of the village on a small hill.

Dedicated to St Peter, the church dates from 1195 and consists of chancel and nave with north and south aisles. entrance is through a door in the lower stage of the tower which is on the south side of the nave.

The two arcades dividing the nave and aisles are of Transitional date, the north arcade being a little older than the south. Each arcade has four pointed arches of two plain chamfered orders with hood mouldings. The piers and responds are cylindrical, those of the south arcade being slightly taller and thinner.

The chancel was rebuilt in 1665 from the old materials when two windows were inserted in its south side. The remaining windows are modern with the exception of a lancet in the south wall west of the tower. The chancel arch was erected about 1860 and replaces a similar one erected in the 12th century. The bench ends in the chancel date from the 17th century. The roof of the nave and chancel is modern and dates from the 19th century.

The tower, which was rebuilt in 1813, contains two bells. Both are inscribed and were cast in 1664 and 1694.

On the outside of the church, over the lancet window in the south wall of the south aisle, there is a much weathered sculptured stone, supposedly representing the Coronation of the Virgin. Part of an incised grave-cover is built into the north wall of the north aisle.

Embleton

Embleton consists of a farm, two ordinary dwelling houses and the church. It derives its name from Elmdene, from an elm-wood which formerly grew in the neighbouring dene.

The church stands on the brink of the dene and during the years landslides have caused the east part of the burial ground to fall into the dene. It is the only remaining one of the four chapels once dependent on the church of Sedgefield.

Dedicated to St Mary, the church has windows all of the lancet type, two in the north wall, three in the south wall and one of three lights in the west end. The east window consists of three lancets. None of the windows contain stained glass. On the west gable is a bell-cot containing one bell. In the sanctuary there is a banner bearing the coat of arms of the Londonderry family.

According to Surtees, the structure has evidently been once extended towards the north as four round arches are closed up in the north wall and it seems probable that the original chancel was also once extended towards the east.

To reach this hamlet one has to go rather off the beaten track and it is probably one of the least visited churches in the county, the nearest place being Elwick Hall.

This church is no longer a place of worship.

Escomb

The village of Escomb lies about two miles west of Bishop Auckland and for the lover of walking is best reached by a path along the south side of the river Wear.

Here is a church which should not be missed, not only because it is the oldest in the county, but probably in the country. It is the most complete and unspoiled example of the Anglo-Saxon church in existence.

The church consists of a small chancel 10 ft each way and a long narrow nave 43½ ft by 14½ ft. A south porch was erected in the 17th century and a bell-cot on the west gable. Most of the stone has been brought from the neighbouring Roman Camp at Binchester. At the top of the walls are a few courses of smaller stones. The corners of the nave and chancel have blocks of stone inserted of especially large size. Near the roof on the north side is a stone inserted upside down with LEG VI carved on it which means the Sixth Roman Legion was probably stationed at Binchester. The bell dates from 1577. In the south wall between the two ancient windows is a Saxon sundial;

there are only three lines to mark the day and it is probably the oldest Saxon sundial in the country.

Inside the church one's attention is arrested by the wonderful chancel arch which is certainly a Roman one brought from Binchester and re-erected. It is 5'3" wide, 11'3", high to the spring and 13'10" to the crown. The stones of the jambs are of the 'long and short' arrangement used by the Anglo-Saxon builders elsewhere.

Traces of wall paintings can be seen on the inner part of the arch and on the north wall of the chancel. In the chancel on the modern window sill above the altar is a pre-Norman stone cross. In the south wall there is a piscina, probably 13th century. The window in the east is modern, 19th century.

In the nave at the west end is a portion of the original stone cobble floor. The font has been altered from a rectangular basin to an irregular octagonal one, and the presence of lockholes show that it once had a cover which would be kept locked to 'prevent witchcraft'. The north and south doors are of Anglo-Saxon workmanship and as often happens are not directly opposite. The original windows are five in number; two are in the south wall, two in the north and one high in the west gable. Those in the south wall and the one in the west gable are round-headed. These windows would be unglazed as the presence of shutter grooves in the jambs indicate this. In the 13th century a long lancet window was inserted in the south wall near the east end and a short one in the chancel. In the 19th century an ugly window was put in the west gable and one in the south wall.

No graves are to be found on the north side of the churchyard as it was customary to avoid burials there, it being regarded as the devil's side as he was supposed to occupy that side of heaven before 'The Fall'.

The nave

Esh

The village of Esh is situated on a high ridge between the Browney and Deerness streams about five miles from Durham. In the middle of the village green stands a stone cross on a pedestal with the inscription IHS on one side and a much worn date, 1687, on the other.

The church stands at the north side of the village green. It is dedicated to St Michael the Archangel and was almost rebuilt in 1770 and then again restored in 1850. The church bell bears the date 1695.

The church consists of a nave with chapel on its south side, and chancel. Entry into the church is by the south porch. The lower parts of most of the walls are ancient.

There are two effigies in the chapel, one lies on a window ledge and is that of an infant in swaddling clothes, the face is broken away. The other, probably late 13th century, is that of a lady and lies at the south end. The hands are folded and the head rests on two cushions. She wears a wimple and the mantle is fastened by a cord. The effigy is probably that of a member of the De Esh Family.

An interesting missal belonging to Esh church can be seen at Ushaw College about two miles east of Esh. The visitor should make every effort to visit this College as it has a museum containing much of local interest and also a fine collection of pictures and statues.

Finchale Priory

The abbey at Finchale is not seen from whichever side it is approached until one is close upon it. There the river makes a rapid bend and nothing can be more pleasant to the eye than the view presented; the steep banks clothed with trees, the river flowing round the foot of the hill and the ancient ruins of Finchale standing amidst all this natural beauty.

In the 12th century St Godric founded a hermitage and when he died, at the age of 105 in 1170, he was buried before the altar in the church of St John.

The erection of the present building commenced at the close of the 12th century. The first part to be built was the choir with its aisles, the two eastern piers of the tower and the arches from the transepts into the choir aisles. Afterwards the north transept was added and this was completed by 1239. The erection of the south transept took place in 1241. During the building of the church, the monastic buildings were being erected.

The church remained, as described, for 100 years. Then it was altered and reduced in size. The aisles of the choir and the north aisle of the nave were dismantled. The arcades of both choir and nave were filled in with masonry and a window was inserted in each bay. The arches from the transepts to the aisles, as well as the opening from the north transept to the apartment on its east side, were treated in the same way. Some very interesting Account Rolls have been preserved relating to these changes which took place from 1364–7.

The choir contains an original lancet window in its north wall. Near the window is a square aumbry. In the south wall is a double piscina and to the west of this a sedilia. The arcades of the choir consist of three arches in each wall, these rest on cylindrical piers. The south arcade capitals are simply moulded whilst those of the north are beautifully carved with leaves and ears of wheat. Of the four piers which carried the tower walls, only the eastern two are contemporary with the choir. The one on the north-west contains the newel stairway by which the tower was reached.

Capital.

The nave has two arcades, each consisting of four arches which rest on piers alternately cylindrical and octagonal.

The west front, like the east gable, had a triplet of lancets and beneath these was the principal entrance to the church. This doorway has an arch of three moulded orders; the inner nook shafts still exist.

The north transept has two tall narrow lancets in its west wall. The south transept has a five-light window in its east wall. Beneath this window stood an altar and in front of this was the tomb of St Godric previously mentioned. To the north of the window is a piscina beneath an ogee-shaped arch.

The monastic buildings stand to the south and west side of the

Cloister. The Refectory is entered from the south of the Cloister by a doorway near the east end. Beneath the Refectory is an undercroft which is vaulted in quadripartite plan with massive transverse and diagonal ribs. The vault rests on five plain octagonal piers and is lighted by six small single lights in the south wall.

The Prior's lodgings are to the south of the choir. They stretch from east to west and have a chapel on the south side. A tower-like structure, known as the Douglas Tower, projects from the east end of the prior's hall on the north side. Its basement has a vaulted apartment. The basement of the prior's buildings is occupied by three vaulted rooms. The vaulting of each of these rooms differs in each case. The east one had barrel vaulting and the middle one plain quadripartite vaulting. The west one, which is much the largest, was vaulted in a much superior manner. Three cylindrical piers along the centre of the room divide it into two aisles. These piers have moulded capitals and bases. The most interesting window in this block of buildings is the now almost destroyed oriel in the north wall. It has been built out on a massive buttress-like projection. The basement of this oriel is popularly known as the Wishing Chair.

Gainford

The lovely village of Gainford stands midway between Darlington and Barnard Castle. Round the village green stand some Georgian houses and at the south-west corner, the church.

The church which is dedicated to St Mary the Virgin, can boast of a close connection to Saxon England. It is first mentioned by Symeon of Durham in AD 801. It consists of chancel, nave with north and south aisles, a western tower and north and south porches. It is almost entirely 13th century.

Entry into the church is by the north porch which is modern. Inserted in its walls are a number of medieval grave-covers. The door is ancient and retains its original hinges. The south porch is also ancient and has side benches.

The nave has arcades on each side, consisting of three pointed arches supported by tall circular piers. The only original windows in the nave are two in the east wall of the south aisle, the lower one being a lancet and the other of vesica-piscis shape. The south wall has four windows filled with Perpendicular tracery, and above them a line of single light windows with ogee-shaped arches. The north wall is similar to the south except that there are only two single light windows with ogee-shaped arches. The tower at the west end is supported by three pointed arches. The font is 13th century with a 17th century oak cover.

The chancel has a pointed arch of two plain chamfered orders. The east window consists of three lancets containing modern glass and above these is a vesica window. In the south wall there are two lancets and between them a priest's door. A door in the north wall leads into the vestry.

Gateshead

Gateshead stands on the south bank of the Tyne, and it was here that one crossed the river by Hadrian's bridge into Northumberland. Today, towering above the church, it is a modern steel bridge, which spans the river. This bridge was the prototype for the Sydney Harbour Bridge in Australia.

There was a church here in the 11th century when Bishop Walcher of Durham was slain outside its doors in 1080 by an infuriated mob. There is some doubt as to whether this church stood on the site of the present one or a little to the east.

The present church, dedicated to St Mary, consists of a chancel, nave with north and south aisles, north and south transepts, a western tower and south porch.

The chancel contains the only ancient parts of the church. These are part of the north wall near the chancel arch, a round-headed window, and eight corbels which support the modern roof. All belong to the Transitional period. The east window is a memorial to the victims of the explosion at Gateshead in 1854. There is an interesting window in the south wall. The chancel floor is very fine with the 121st Psalm inscribed on its tiles. There is also an elaborately carved gravestone, dated 1684, in the floor.

The north transept was built in Perpendicular times and in the east wall of the south transept are two blocked Perpendicular windows

The nave has a 15th century roof which bears along its centre some very good bosses carved with foliage. The nave is divided from the aisles by arcades of five arches which spring from octagonal piers without capitals, but having moulded bosses (14th century). The clerestory belongs to this period but its windows are entirely modern, like all the other windows in the church. There is a gallery over the north and south aisles.

The present tower was built in 1740, and the west end of the nave dates from then. The basement of the tower is now the Baptistry. To the south of the tower arch we find an old engraving of the church done in lead, dated 1749, and to the north of the arch a picture by Charles le Brun, 'The Descent from the Cross', painted on copper. A larger copy of this picture hangs in Rennes Cathedral in France. Beside this picture is a wooden tablet bearing details of the 1854 explosion.

The south doorway of the nave is of Transitional date, the only original part being the moulded arch. The porch contains some ancient grave-covers. An old Saxon cross stands against the wall. There is a memorial cross on the east wall which was originally erected on the Somme battlefield in 1916.

There are some interesting show cases in the church. An ancient Churchwardens' seat, dated 1666 stands within the chancel screen. Two black oak chests, dated 1647, have four locks each which could only be opened when all the church-wardens were present. The choir stalls were erected in 1695. The church clock was built in 1755 and still has its original works.

The churchyard has had no internments since 1854 when 140 people were buried there after an outbreak of cholera. Near the priest's door stands an old stone coffin. At the east end of the south transept there can be seen a collection of stones which were blown onto the roof of the church in the 1854 explosion. On the north side of the chancel and over the vestries is a large room known as The Anchorage. This was built as a result of a grant in 1340 from the Bishop of Durham to the Rector of Brancepeth 'to build an habitation for an anchoress'. Of its original purpose we know nothing. It is first mentioned in 1693 when it was in use as a school.

This church is now redundant and used for commercial purposes.

Churchwarden's chair, 1666.

Greatham

The village of Greatham is about six miles from Stockton. On its south-west side, amidst a cluster of trees, we find the Parish Church, and adjoining it Greatham Hospital, originally a hospital for lepers, like that at Sherburn.

The church, dedicated to St John the Baptist, is modern, with the exception of the arcades in the nave. It consists of nave with side aisles, chancel, a western tower, and a south porch.

The font is of marble and belongs to the Transitional period. The altar stone is also of Frosterley marble and is pre-Reformation.

Of the original edifice, only the four western bays of the arcades remain. The north arcade is Transitional. The arches are pointed and are of two orders; the first and second piers from the east are cylindrical and the third is octagonal. The original part of the south arcade consists of pointed arches with two plain chamfered orders. The piers are similar to those of the north.

There are several sculptured stones of an early date built into the north walls of the nave, and fragments of ancient crosses lie on the floor. Some of these bear the star ornament which dates from the reign of Henry I.

Great Stainton

The village of Great Stainton, approximately five miles from Sedgefield and four miles from Sadberge, stands on a hill on the old Roman road from York to Newcastle. That it was a much larger place than it is today, can be seen from traces of foundations still visible in the surrounding fields.

The church, dedicated to All Saints, was entirely rebuilt in 1876, but it stands on the site of a Norman church. Its spire is a notable landmark for miles around.

Built into the interior walls of the tower are several 17th century tombstones and fragments of medieval grave-covers with the usual decoration of carved crosses. The font is the original Norman one and has an octagonal bowl.

Outside in the churchyard there is an unusual tombstone; it is a stone shaft terminating in a carved hand which has its index finger pointing to heaven.

Grindon

The ruined church of Grindon stands about 1/4 of a mile east of the Sedgefield – Stockton road, approximately 2 miles north of Thorpe Thewles.

Dedicated to St Thomas à Becket, the church ceased to be a place of worship when the present church at Thorpe Thewles was erected in the 19th century. The altar stone at Thorpe Thewles comes from Grindon as does the coped stone coffin of Roger de Fulthorpe in the churchyard. The name Grindon probably means 'Green Hill'.

Most of the building is of squared stones but the greater part of the north wall is of brickwork, probably done when the church was practically rebuilt in 1788. The nave has two original lancet windows in the south wall, one in the north and one in the west end.

The south doorway, probably 13th century date, is a pointed arch of two orders with a roll moulding on the angle of each. The west gable is capped by a bell-cot. Opposite the south door can be seen a walled-in doorway. An arched brick recess in the nave was once the fireplace of the pew belonging to the owners of Wynyard Hall.

The remains of a chapel on the south side of the chancel is an addition of the Decorated period and was known as the Fulthorpe Porch. There is a piscina at the east end of the south wall. The steps from the nave into the chancel are still visible, but all the floor of the interior is covered in rubble and overgrown with grass.

The churchyard contains very few gravestones and has been surrounded by a stone wall, but now has a wooden fence.

Surtees in his history writes 'Near the centre of the floor are 2 blue slabs laid closely together. The one has a sword suspended from a cross and just above the hilt of the sword the cross moline of Fulthorpe; the other stone has only a cross. During excavations two ponderous oak coffins were discovered at a depth of 6 ft fast decaying under the latter stone.'

Hamsterley

The village of Hamsterley stands on a high ridge, about seven miles from Bishop Auckland and two and a half miles from Witton-le-Wear.

The church of St James, lying about half a mile east of the village, is built in the cruciform plan with a south porch and a western bell-turret. Entrance into the church is by the 13th century porch, its doorway being simple Norman work.

The only ancient window in the nave is the western one, this is square-headed. The nave is divided from the chancel and transepts by pointed arches. The chancel arch is plain chamfered of one order resting on corbels. The north and south transepts arches have been rebuilt.

The east window, consisting of a triplet of lancets, is modern. In the south wall there are two lancets, one is ancient. There is a square aumbry on the north side and a trefoil-headed piscina with a circular projecting basin on the south.

The Early English window in the north wall of the north transept is the finest architectural feature of the church.

The south transept has a triplet of lancets in its south wall; these have been restored.

During restorations several grave-covers were discovered and these, together with others which were previously in the church, have been inserted into the walls.

Outside the church the visitor sees something very unusual. Two weather worn monuments which lie side by side appear to have had the west wall of the south transept built across them, but the monuments are of a later date than the wall, therefore, this must have been pierced in order to place them in their present position. Why this has been done remains a mystery.

Hart

The village of Hart stands on the brow of a hill commanding a fine view of the town of Hartlepool and the coast, four miles distant.

The church of St Mary Magdalene, mother church of Hartlepool, consists of chancel, nave with north and south aisles, a western tower, and a south porch. Parts of the building are of pre-Conquest date, evidence of which is visible in the voussoirs over the chancel arch and the triangular-headed opening above them. The church was originally aisle-less.

The nave on its north side has two wide round arches (15th century), each having three chamfered orders resting on an octagonal pier with moulded capitals and bases. This arcade was pierced through the earlier wall, and the corbel table seen in the north aisle was originally exterior. The corbels are grotesque heads of early Norman date. The south arcade has four obtuse pointed arches with octagonal piers of the Decorated period. The south aisle contains a piscina near the east of its south wall. A collection of stones of various dates, found during restorations in 1890, lies at the west end of the south aisle. Excepting those at Jarrow and Monkwearmouth, the two lathe baluster shafts are unique in the North.

The south doorway and porch are of the same date as the south arcade.

The chancel arch is 15th century, it is round-headed and is of three chamfered orders resting on semi-octagonal responds.

The Norman tower consists of three stages and opens to the nave with a round arch of one order. In the south and west walls of the lowest stage there is a lancet window.

The Tower Arch and Font.

The church contains two fonts: one is Norman, a cylindrical basin hollowed out of one square stone, on each angle is carved a cylindrical shaft with a cushion capital; the other font is Perpendicular and is the most ornate example to be found in the county. On the south side of its bowl are carved the figures of St Barnabas, holding a staff in his right hand, and St Jude, holding a book in his right hand and a boat in the left. On the south-east side is the figure of an ox, emblem of St Luke. On the east side St James holds in his right hand a book and in his left, a club. St Philip holds in his right hand a book and three loaves in the left. On the north-east side, we see a winged man, emblem of St Matthew. On the north, St Thomas and St Simon; north-west, winged lion, emblem of St Mark; west, The Resurrection; at right, three nails and crown of thorns, at left, the scourge, spear and a sponge on a reed. An eagle, emblem of St John. On its shaft – South, St Appolonia. South-east, a Pope with triple crown. East, St Euphemia. North-east, St Othilia. North, St Barbara. North-west, a bishop. West, St Elizabeth. South-west, an abbot.

Outside, on the south wall of the chancel there is a much weathered sculptured stone of St George and the Dragon. The angle quoins of the original aisle-less nave are visible at the south-east and north-east corners.

Hartlepool

St Hilda's at Old Hartlepool perhaps the finest parish church in the county, was once a chapel-of-ease to the mother church at Hart The church is remarkable in being of nearly all one period very Early English, with the exception of some Transitional work, and a Norman south door.

The most striking aspect from the outside is the massive western buttressed tower, and the clerestory, which is arcaded with a triplet of arches in each bay, the central one being a window.

The most breathtaking view on the inside are the arcades of the nave, six arches on each side. The south arcade is a little earlier than that of the north. The piers are clustered columns supporting pointed arches. The south side has hood mouldings with the nutmeg ornament. The aisle windows are renewed Perpendicular windows, with the exception of lancets, also renewed on the south side of the chancel aisle. These aisles extend from the nave right into the chancel.

The tower stands on four supporting columns. The weight of the tower on its shallow foundations caused it to slip as can be seen by the column next to it on the south side, which also accounts for the massive buttresses supporting the outside walls.

The chancel was rebuilt in 1925 but on the original foundations as near as possible to the original design. Behind the altar is the Brus Chapel containing one of the tombs to the Bruce family, who originally built the church in 1185.

The Galilee Chapel is behind the west door in the tower; this was restored in 1930 and is the only example of this type of chapel in the county except perhaps for that at Sadberge.

At the east end of the north aisle there is a collection of ancient stones; the oldest is a Saxon arch; the most interesting a 14th century gravestone on which is carved a sailing ship. On the wall is an Elizabethan brass to one Jane Bell who died in 1593.

In the south wall of the south aisle there is a piscina, and a walled up priest's door gives evidence of this having once been a chantry.

A convent was founded at Hartlepool by St Heui in AD 640 who succeeded St Hilda in AD 649. This building was completely destroyed by the Danes in AD 800. In 1833 about 135 yards south-east of the present church, close to the present swimming pool, the ancient cemetery of the earlier church was discovered.

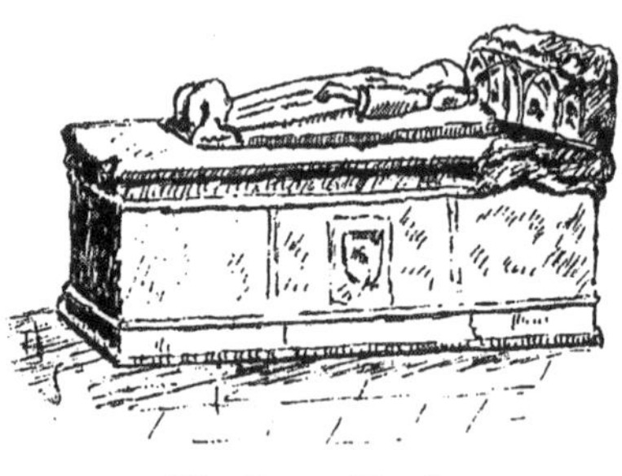

The Bruce Tomb.

Haughton-le-Skerne

The village of Haughton-le-Skerne is about a mile and a half north-east of Darlington. The church is situated on a slope by Salter's Lane which stands on the old Salt Road which ran from Newcastle to London.

The church, dedicated to St Andrew, consists of chancel, nave with north and south transepts, a western tower, and a south porch. The oldest parts of the building date from 1135. Entrance is by the south porch which is modern. In its walls are fragments of ancient grave-covers. The doorway is a plain arch of one square order covering a plain tympanum. The hood moulding is decorated with the billet ornament.

A window in the north wall of the nave has been blocked with Saxon and other carved stones. The box pews are Jacobean, the doors still retaining their iron latches. On the north wall there are three escutcheons, one that of George II, dated 1757, another to a late rector of the church, an uncle of Lord Byron, and buried in the churchyard, and the third, dated 1790, to a late benefactoress of the church, whose portrait can be seen in the vestry. The north doorway has been blocked and placed against it are several carved stones, one of which bears three dragons' heads and arrows. This design is to be found carved on the back of one of the chairs standing in the Sanctuary.

The transepts were added in the 19th century. The south transept contains several old relics including an old chest and some iron candlesticks, once used in the lighting of the church.

The chancel arch consists of two plain square orders with another opening above. On each side of the arch there have been two large openings, hagioscopes. A monumental brass on the wall beside the

The pulpit.

north opening is dated 1592. On the south side of the chancel arch is the pulpit and on the north a reading desk, each one having a massive sounding board. The chancel was originally lighted by round-headed windows, traces of which are still visible. A square-headed priest's door, now blocked, is in the north wall and opposite is a low-side Perpendicular window, also blocked. The piscina in the south wall of the Sanctuary and the aumbry in the north, are still in use. In the Canon's stall there is a carving of a bird, and the date 1649, very rudely done.

The tower is very unusual. Its ground plan is not square and it is not placed in the centre of the west front of the church. The west doorway into the tower has a plain round-headed arch of one order, and nook shafts with cushioned capitals. The upper stages of the tower are reached by a newel stair enclosed in a turret on the south side. In the base of the tower there is the font, its shaft and base dating from the 12th century. On the floor is an inscribed stone slab. The tower contains four bells, one which is pre-Reformation is an alphabet bell, the only one in the county.

In 1748 a farmer, named Colling, saw a fine bull passing the church. Seeking its owner, he bought it for 8 guineas. From this bull he bred a small herd and from this in turn is descended one of the world's great breeds, the Shorthorn.

Heighington

The village of Heighington stands on a large hill with the houses clustering round a large green sloping gradually to the south.

The church stands at the north side of the green and from its tower one can see a considerable part of the southern half of the county and part of North Yorkshire. Dedicated to St Michael the Archangel, the church consists of a chancel, nave with north and south aisles, a western tower, and a south porch. Its oldest portions are early Norman.

Entrance into the church is through the south porch which has fragments of ancient grave-covers in its walls. The doorway is part of the old church and was originally on the north side of the building. It has a semicircular arch resting on round shafts, these have been restored. The south aisle is Early English and has an arcade of three pointed arches resting on octagonal piers. There is a piscina in the south wall.

The tower is early Norman and is in three stages. The parapet was added in the 15th century and has a grotesque gargoyle at each corner. Standing in the base of the tower is the old eight-sided font and, nearby, three medieval grave-covers and the effigies of two females (14th century). The belfry contains six bells, three form the original peal (probably 15th century).

The chancel arch is semi-circular and is of two orders. In the north wall there are two ancient windows; one is blocked and only visible in the vestry. A medieval memorial, a grave-cover with a floriated cross, stands against the north wall and, near to this, there is a white marble monument to Captain William Pryce Cumby who fought at Trafalgar aboard the *Bellerophon* as its Lieutenant and took over command of the ship when the captain was killed. He died at Pembroke on the 17th September 1837.

The most remarkable object in the church is the medieval oak pulpit, the only one in the county. It has six panels, each filled in the upper part with tracery, below these the linen pattern is carved, and a Latin inscription is carved round the cornice.

Houghton-le-Spring

The church of St Michael is of cruciform plan, consisting of chancel, nave with north and south aisles, north and south transepts and a tower at the intersection. It is mainly Early English.

The nave is separated from the aisles by arcades of pointed arches of two plain chamfered orders resting on columns consisting of eight cylindrical shafts, four large ones, with four smaller ones intervening. The capitals are unusual, projecting beyond the piers, the section of which they follow. These fine arcades are the only original features of the nave. The clerestory contains no windows and apparently never has. The restored west window, filled with graceful tracery, is 14th century. The south doorway is a restoration and the porch is modern.

The transepts open to the aisles of the nave by arches of one order. The east walls of both transepts have tall lancets. The south transept has three and the north two; the organ chamber replaces the third. The windows in the gables of each transept are modern. In the west wall of both transepts there are two windows each consisting of two lancets. These are of great interest for they show the first attempts of

13th century architects to use the space between, and above, the arches of two adjoining lancets. The arches are cut in a single stone. The south transept contains various monuments of interest. In the base of the west gable there is a recess crowned with a segmental arch containing an effigy of a knight, much weathered (late 13th century). Another effigy in a much better state of preservation lies on the floor and nearby is the altar tomb of the famed Bernard Gilpin, the 'Apostle of the North', who died in 1583.

A brass on the east wall to one Margery Belassis who died in 1587, portrays her with her family of eight sons and four daughters. There are two piscinas, one in the south wall of this transept and the other in the east wall of the north transept.

The tower walls rest on four arches opening to the chancel, nave, and north and south transepts. The arches which are pointed, are of two plain chamfered orders and rest on semi-octagonal responds with richly moulded capitals. The lower stage of the tower is of the same date as the arches. The upper stage which is battlemented is entirely modern and replaces a steeple.

The chancel contains some Norman work. The north wall has a round-headed window and, to the west of this, a very narrow square-headed doorway, with two winged monsters interlaced, carved on its tympanum. The south wall has an arcade of eight lancet windows. This has been restored and its two east windows and the west one are modern. A doorway in the south wall is square-headed within and pointed without.

A detached two-storeyed building on the south side of the chancel was built for the purpose of a Guild established in 1476. The room in the basement is now used as a vestry. The upper room has a three light window in the south wall and a two light square-headed window in the east wall. On this side there is a chimney shaft corbelled out of the wall. This room would, no doubt, be for the housing of the incumbent of the guild. That the building was in direct communication with the church is certain. A corridor links it with the church and from it one can enter the chancel by the south door or the south transept by a door in the east wall.

Across the road west of the church stands the Rectory. In its grounds there is an old hawthorn kept together by iron bands and known as Bernard Gilpin's thorn. The ancient Almshouses at the east end of the churchyard were founded by George Lilburn. Houghton

Hall, a 17th century building, on the right of the road which passes the church on its south side, is now used as a club. In the garden stands an altar tomb to Robert Hutton, who had a troop of horses under his command in Cromwell's army. He was a staunch Puritan which probably accounts for his being buried here. He died in 1681.

Hurworth-on-Tees

The church of All Saints stands in the middle of the village. On its north side lies the village street and on its south the river Tees. The present church was rebuilt in 1870. The only part of the ancient edifice is the two bays of each arcade in the nave and these have been re-erected from the old materials. The arches are pointed and are of two chamfered orders. The central piers are cylindrical and the others octagonal and the capitals are moulded following the sections of the piers.

In the basement of the tower are two sepulchral effigies of Knights. The oldest of these is similar to those found at Chester-le-Street, Pittington and Whitworth. The effigies were probably brought from the neighbouring Neasham Abbey and are of the 13th century.

The church has north and south transepts and an aisle on the north side of the chancel. On the window ledges in both transepts are carved stone heads, probably gargoyles from the old church. The interior walls of the chancel are of a mauve tinted sandstone giving the effect of having been painted. There are several memorials in the church which is clean and well lit by stained glass windows. The choir stalls are fashioned from oak taken from the Rectory Tithe Barn which was dismantled in 1880.

In the churchyard are the remains of a native of the village who rose from a humble position to be a captain in the Life Guards and was present at the Battle of Waterloo. Here also is the tomb of William Emerson an eccentric mathematician who dies in 1782 at the age of 81. He was the author of many mathematical works and refused a membership of the Royal Society.

In 1645 the village of Hurworth was hit by a terrible plague which affected many parts of England, in the month of July 340 deaths occurred from this awful scourge in this parish alone.

Carefully preserved in the church is the register 1559–1715. In it are records of all the burials during the plague. The rector at that time himself caught the infection, and on July 18th 1645, he died and was buried.

Jarrow

The town of Jarrow, like many others on the Wear and Tyne, it is an industrial one. It was here in AD 681 that Benedict Biscop founded a monastery in which the Venerable Bede lived from the age of seven years until his death on the 26th May 735. Bede, one of the greatest scholars of his day, wrote some of the finest literature in the English language yet with the exception of occasional visits to the neighbouring monastery at Monkwearmouth he never travelled.

Today, the church of St Paul's consists of a chancel, central tower, nave with north aisle and a western porch. The oldest parts of the building are the chancel and tower, both containing pre-Conquest work.

The lowest stages of the tower are Saxon, the upper stage very early Norman. In plan the tower is unusual and remarkable in the fact that it is twice as long on the north and south sides as on the east and west sides. In the lowest stages there are four round-headed openings, as at Monkwearmouth, which lead into the nave, chancel and vestry. The south one is blocked. Above the western arch is a most remarkable object, viz. the original dedication stone of the church. This was found in 1783 during the rebuilding of the nave. Translated it reads, 'The dedication of the basilica of St Paul on the 9th of the kalends of May in the 15th year of King Ecgfrid and the 4th of Abbot Ceolfrid founder under God of the said church.' The nave was again rebuilt in 1866. A collection of baluster shafts and other ancient fragments of stonework lie in the north porch.

The chancel which was originally the nave dates from Saxon times. There are three of the original small round-headed windows in the south wall, two of these blocked in the upper part with stone slabs pierced with a round hole to admit the light. There is a blocked round-headed Saxon doorway in the north wall. The choir stalls contain four lovely 15th century bench ends carved with tracery; the western finial bears the badge of Prior Thomas Castell (1494–1519). In the sanctuary stands a chair commonly known as Bede's chair but which is more probably 14th century.

To many people the name Jarrow conjured up to the mind the days of the Great Depression during the early 1930s when its men marched to London on their 'Hunger Marches'.

Bede's Chair.

Kelloe

Kelloe church is about two miles from Trimdon. It stands in a secluded valley on the north side of Kelloe beck, unfortunately now encroached on by the neighbouring colliery.

Dedicated to St Helen, the church consists of chancel, nave with a chapel on the north side, south porch and a western tower. The chancel is Early English. There is a lancet window in the north wall and a doorway originally external now leading into the vestry. In the sanctuary are three medieval grave-covers and a Norman cross. This cross was found in fragments in the walls of the old chancel and is beautifully and accurately sculptured. It consists of three panels and the subject is that of the finding of the Cross on Mount Calvary by the Empress Helena (St Helen), mother of Constantine the Great. At the four arms of the cross and in its central boss are cavities, five in all, intended to hold relics and a little below the centre cavity a contrivance probably intended to hold candles before the principal relic.

The east window which is of three lights belonging to the

Decorated period has been renewed. There is a piscina in a plain square recess. The chancel arch is of two plain chamfered orders. The chapel on the north side of the nave, Thornlaw Porch as it was called, was founded by John Fitz Henry de Kellaw and his sister, Elizabeth, in 1347. It has a two light window of Perpendicular date filled with stained glass as a memorial to the Trimdon Grange Mine disaster. The chapel was the burial place of the possessors of Thornley and was much larger than it is today.

Norman cross, c.1200.

The chancel was taken down and rebuilt in 1854. The south door is early Norman, the shafts having been destroyed. The tower, which is Norman, is supported by large buttresses and opens to the nave by a pointed arch of two chamfered orders. The abaci of the original tower arch can be seen. In the belfry are two bells, one being inscribed. On the outside of the tower is a much weathered sundial. The porch has been added later and is of uncertain date. Above it is a round-headed window now blocked in. In the exterior of the north wall of the nave can be seen some herringbone masonry.

The church has two memorials relating to Coxhoe Hall, now demolished, both on the south side of the nave. One is a plaque which states that Elizabeth Barrett Browning was born there. In the register kept in the vestry can be seen the entry of her birth, also that of one of her brothers. The other memorial is a stained glass window to the Wood family, last owners of Coxhoe Hall.

In the churchyard the gravestones have been removed and lined up against the north wall. In the north-east corner lies the family vault of the Woods. In the new churchyard is a memorial to a mine disaster at Trimdon Grange Colliery on 16th February 1882. Here lie buried 26 of the 74 men and boys who lost their lives.

The names of the early Rectors of the church are lost but the list of Vicars is fairly complete from the 13th century. The first curate was in 1578.

Kirk Merrington

The church, dedicated to St John the Evangelist, stands 642 ft above sea-level on one of the highest hills in the county and commanding one of its finest views. It was rebuilt and enlarged in 1851, the only original part to be retained being the north wall of the chancel. The church, which is a copy of the original, consists of nave, tower, chancel and north transept. The square tower resting on round arches is in the centre, a common feature of Norman churches. Carved grotesque faces peer out from underneath the parapet. It was commonly believed that these warded off evil spirits and that the sins of the congregation escaped from the church through their mouths.

Entrance to the church is by the south door which consists of three orders of carved chevron. It is set in a shallow porch which contains several ancient coped grave-covers, two bearing the tile pattern. A 13th century grave-cover bearing the symbols of a spade and sword has traditionally been ascribed to Roger-de-Ferry who slew the wild boar of Brancepeth at Cleves Cross about two miles east of Merrington.

The nave consists of three arches with zig-zag pattern and is separated from the chancel by a richly carved oak screen of the 17th century as at Sedgefield.

The chancel contains three box pews of carved oak with poppy-head bench ends. The altar is a massive oak table of late 17th century date and is somewhat unusual in the fact that it stands a considerable distance from the east wall. The square shaped box pew on the north side belonged to the Eden family late owners of Windlestone Hall.

The font (of unknown date) which is made of sandstone and very weatherbeaten, lay in pieces for many years in the vicarage garden.

The church was besieged and garrisoned during the rebellion of the Usurper William Cumin in 1143 and a trench of uncoffined bones discovered in the churchyard probably dates from that time.

In the churchyard near the south wall of the church stands a most remarkable altar tomb to some children named Brass, who were murdered at a nearby farm by a servant in 1683. Two words viz. 'was executed' were erased long ago by means of a stick used by an old man who visited the grave each day. One John Stokoe, a surgeon in the RN who attended Napoleon on St Helena, is also buried in this churchyard.

The belfry contains two bells dated 1723 and 1729.

On a clear day it is well worth climbing to the top of the tower for the view over on the south-east, one can see the North Sea and ships entering and leaving the mouth of the Tees, to the north, Durham Cathedral and beyond, Penshaw Monument. On the south side the plain of Durham stretches to Darlington and thence to York.

Inscription on the altar tomb:-

Here lie the bodies
of John, Jane and Elizabeth
children of
John and Margaret Brass
who were murdered on the 25th January 1683
by Andrew Mills their Father's servant
for which he .... and hung in chains.
Reader remember sleeping we were slain
And here we sleep till we must rise again
Who so sheddeth man's blood
By man shall his blood be shed.
Thou shalt do no murder.
Restored by Subscription 1789.

Lamesley

The village of Lamesley is situated two and a half miles west of Birtley not far from the Team Valley Trading Estate. A church existed here before 1286 as a Chapel-of-Ease to the church at Chester-le-Street but the present building, dedicated to St Andrew, is entirely modern, dating from 1759. Its square tower with an octagonal turret on the north-east corner was added in 1821.

The nave has side aisles and the four pointed arches resting on clustered pillars on each side of the nave go to the full height of the building. There are galleries in the upper half of the aisles which are reached by short spiral stairways. A grave-cover with a carved cross and a pair of shears lies in the south-east corner of the nave. Two stones belonging to the early church lie near to the font at the west end of the building.

The chancel contains numerous memorials to the Liddells, owners of the late castle of Ravensworth. The most imposing is a monument in memory of Frances Jane Liddell, who died November, 1823, aged 24. It shows a mourning woman leaning over an altar with a little putto at the opposite side.

In the churchyard close to the vestry is the grave of John Croft, Vicar of Lamesley from 1898 to 1951. He died in 1951, aged 100 years. His wife, who is buried with him was 97 and died in 1952. They celebrated their 75th Wedding Anniversary in 1950.

Lanchester

The village of Lanchester is about eight miles north-west of Durham and lies in a sheltered vale through which runs Smallhope Burn, a tributary of the Browney. About half a mile south-west of the village stands the site of a Roman station.

The church is of great interest, consisting of chancel with ancient vestry, nave with north and south aisles, a south porch and western tower. The oldest portions are Norman (or Roman?). The chancel arch is Norman and consists of three orders adorned with chevron mouldings. The most remarkable feature about it is the height of the base of its jambs above the floors of both nave and chancel. The bases of the shafts are over 6 ft above the floor of the nave. The chancel floor must have been considerably higher than the nave like that at Barnard Castle church.

The chancel was rebuilt in the 13th century. The remaining original windows are the three lancets in the east wall and three in the north wall which are now blocked. Within the altar rails there are corbels carved with human heads each having a bracket intended for candles.

The recesses in the side walls of the chancel have arches of four orders. The south recess is partly occupied by a large beautiful window of three lights, containing stained glass of Early English date, one piece of great interest being the Flight into Egypt. The doorway into the vestry has a cinquefoil arch with a representation of Our Lord in Session, on the tympanum. A brass on the floor of the chancel is to John Rudd, a Dean of Lanchester, who died in 1490. A 13th century piscina with a niche behind it, projects from the south wall. The misericords at the west end of the choir stalls on the south side are 15th century.

Roman altar about A.D.244. Lanchester Church.

The nave clerestory was added during the 16th century. The nave roof also dates from then. The arcades into the north and south aisles are Transitional, each consists of four arches. The arches of the north side are pointed and rest on cylindrical monolithic pillars, originally arcade pillars from the Roman station. The south arches are similar in design, but were rebuilt in the 14th century.

The effigy of a priest (probably 14th century) lies in a recess at the east end of the south aisle. He holds a chalice and is attired in alb, chasuble, stole and maniple. His head rests on a cushion and his feet on a lamb.

The south porch dates from the 13th century. Its roof has ribbed vaulting. Against the east wall stands a Roman altar (dated about AD 244) which was found locally. The inner south doorway has the original 700 years old ironwork on the door.

The present tower was built about 1430. It consists of three stages and is embattled with pinnacles at each corner. The lowest stage has a good example of ribbed vaulting of the Decorated period. There is a Royal Coat of Arms over the tower arch, dated 1767. The belfry contains six bells.

The church plate has a chalice cover which bears an inscription of the date of its discovery in the ruins of the Roman Station, viz. 1571.

Long Newton

Long Newton, a straggling village of about half a mile in length, lies about a mile beyond Elton.

The church is entirely modern, having been rebuilt in 1857 in the style known locally as the Barrington. It consists of nave and chancel with a vaulted mausoleum to the Vane family on the north side. Many years ago the Vanes had their family mansion at Long Newton. On the mausoleum walls are memorial plaques to this family, perhaps the most noticeable one being to the third Marquess of Londonderry. This Marquess was a General in the army, the founder of Seaham Harbour and the first Lieutenant of the County of Durham. A memorial to this distinguished figure is seen by thousands of people every year in Durham market place, viz. a statue of him dressed in full military dress and seated on his horse.

A brass to Sir George Vane dated 1679 reads:-

Here lieth the body of Sr George Vane interred
May the first 1679 Second son of Sr Henery
Vane sometime Principall Secretary of State

To King Charles the First He Married Elizabeth
The Heiresse of Sr Lyonell Maddison of New
Castle Vpon Tyne, By whom he had thirteene
Hopefvll children, viz. fovre sons and nine davghters
His honovr wonne ith feild lies here ith dost
His honovr got by grace shall never rvst
The former fades the latter shall faile never
For why, he was Sr George once bvt St George ever.

Low Dinsdale

The village of Dinsdale is 'far from the madding crowd' and lies beside a bend in the river Tees about five miles from Darlington. Today it is a small sleepy village but in 1789 a sulphur spring was discovered there and from then on, for approximately eight years, it became quite famous as possessing waters of healing powers.

The church, almost hidden by trees, stands near the bridge which crosses the Tees here into Yorkshire. It is dedicated to St John and consists of chancel, nave with a south aisle, a south porch and a western tower. The tower was added in 1875 when the church was restored with red sandstone.

The arcade which divides the nave from the aisle is of two bays, with pointed arches resting on an octagonal pier. In the south aisle is a Norman font no longer used. A hogbacked grave-cover, carved with interlacing work on the sides and with the head of a boar at one end, lies by the lectern.

The chancel arch is of two plain chamfered orders and has neither responds nor corbels.

There are two piscinae, one in the south wall of the chancel and the other in the aisle which is a restoration.

The south porch is modern but has built into its walls several fragments of pre-Conquest crosses. There is a grave-cover of 14th century date bearing an incised cross and sword and the inscription 'GOSELYNUS SURTEES'. This is no doubt the grave-cover of Goseline Surtees who died in 1366. Dinsdale was the ancient home of the Surtees who settled here after the Conquest and the family seems to have taken its name from the river – 'sur Tees'.

Outside in the churchyard there is a stone coffin nearly six feet long which has a coped lid carved with a raised cross along its full length.

Medomsley

The village of Medomsley stands on a high ridge overlooking the Derwent valley about three miles from Consett and two from Ebchester.

The church, dedicated to St Mary Magdalene, was greatly restored in 1878, and has, as so often happens, lost a lot of its original beauty. It consists of a chancel, with a vestry on the north side, nave with north aisle, and south porch. There is a bell-cot on the west gable. Before the restorations the church was an exceedingly long flat-roofed building. Pictures of it can be seen in the porch and vestry.

The chancel is the most interesting part of the whole building. The east window consists of a triplet of lancets. The shafts have moulded capitals, bands mid-way, and bases. The internal arch mouldings of these windows are modern. In the south wall there is a trefoiled Early English piscina. To the west of this are a piscina and aumbry under a lintel which belonged to the chancel before it was extended eastwards during the 13th century. Two carved heads are near the east end of each of the side walls. Fixed on the top of one of them remains an iron spike on which candles used to be fixed. There are two original windows in the south wall of the chancel, the western one is a modern insertion. The chancel arch is 13th century of two chamfered orders and rests on moulded corbels; the north corbel is original whilst the one on the south is a copy.

The nave was extended eastwards at the same time as the chancel, viz. the 13th century. This extension encroached on the western part of the old chancel. The nave lost nearly all its original features during the recent restorations with the exception of the south door. This has a round-headed arch of two orders with chamfered label. The north wall has a modern arcade of arches for its full length pierced by windows at regular intervals. The arches dividing the nave from the north aisle have cylindrical shafts with round capitals ornamented with the same design as that on the corbels of the chancel arch and are late 19th century. The east window is a long lancet and is an insertion in an earlier wall. This can be clearly seen outside as a buttress has been cut down to accommodate the great length of the window.

On the floor beside the pulpit there is a coped grave-cover bearing an inscription and part of another. The south porch contains fragments of carved stones from the original church. The nave and chancel have their original finials on each respective gable.

Head in chancel.

Middleton-in-Teesdale

The church of St Mary the Virgin is modern, having been built in 1886. It stands hidden among the trees at the west end of the village. Fragments of grave-covers are built into the north wall of the nave; two of these are grave-covers of children whilst the remainder bear crosses; one has a shield carved beneath the mount. A two-light window in the organ chamber belongs to the Decorated period. There is a cinquefoil headed piscina in the vestry and in the north wall of the Sanctuary a memorial brass, dated 1620. The basin of the font which is modern is supported by four shafts; the central one being modern and the others ancient and rudely carved.

The church is the only one of its kind in the County having a detached bell-tower. This stands in the north-west corner of the churchyard and was probably built about the middle of the 16th century. It is of two storeys with a low pitched roof and windows in each gable. There are three bells.

The scenery round about Middleton-in-Teesdale is the wildest and most lovely in the county.

Middleton St George

The parish of Middleton St George is about five miles south-east of Darlington. The houses which stand above the Tees are known as Middleton-one-Row and it is to this lovely spot that visitors flock at week-ends.

The old parish church of St George stands in a field almost hidden by trees about a mile to the south-east of Middleton-one-Row.

It consists of chancel, nave with south porch and a western tower. The tower was added in 1883 in memory of one of the Cocks of the Manor House which lies to the south of the church. Towards the end of the 18th century the nave was enlarged on the north side and the chancel rebuilt. The original width of the nave is marked on the east wall. The chancel arch is 13th century and consists of two chamfered orders. The inner order rests on corbel heads. The north one is of a smiling man and the south one is of a woman putting out her tongue, no doubt at the man opposite. The font, probably Norman, is a plain round basin of pink stones. Stained glass in the east window depicts St George, the church's patron

Saint. The window in the south wall of the chancel bears a coat-of-arms.

Fragments of two grave-covers lie outside against the south wall of the nave. One bears a fine piece of carving whilst the other is much weathered.

The church at Middleton-one-Row is a 19th century building, but it has two antiquities from the old parish church of St George. These are a Saxon sundial and a grave-cover in two halves.

Monk Hesleden

The village of Monk Hesleden is somewhat off the beaten track and consists of church, vicarage, Hesleden Hall and a few cottages.

The church of St Mary stands on the brink of Hesleden Dene in a very charming and romantic spot. It consists of chancel, nave and a bell-turret over the west gable. The oldest part of the church is the south doorway which is early Norman. The arch is rounded of one square order resting on chamfered abaci beneath which are nook-shafts with plain capitals and bases. In the north wall of the chancel there are two walled-up pointed arches of 13th century date. In the south wall of the nave there is a three-light Early English window now blocked and traces of a second window of a similar type. The east window is modern and the only other windows are sashed ones belonging to the 18th century.

The font, 17th century, is an oval basin of sandstone.

There are two bells in the turret, both are pre-Reformation and are supposed to be early 16th century.

The churchyard is somewhat overgrown but nevertheless the whole place has a feeling of peace and tranquillity about it.

The church was demolished 1966.

Monkwearmouth

The parish of Monkwearmouth lies on the north bank of the river Wear. All that remains of the ancient monastery which was built there in AD 674 by Benedict Biscop is the church of St Peter, consisting of chancel, nave with north aisle, north transept and western tower; the oldest parts are the chancel and tower. In AD 866 the greater part of the church was destroyed by the Danish pirates, Hubba and Hingmar; the blackened walls of the porch under the tower are grim reminders of this raid. The church is thought to be the first in England to have windows filled with glass.

The tower, built onto the porch, is Saxon and probably dates from the latter part of the 9th century. It has four round-headed doorways in its lowest stage. The baluster shafts which support the arch of the western door are the only shafts still remaining in their original positions in any Saxon church. The barrel vaulted roof of the porch is also the only example of this type of Saxon work to be found in England. Beneath the baluster shafts are two long flat stones which have entwined serpents carved on them.

The nave, with the exception of the west wall, is 19th century. The west wall was probably built a little before the tower as it is not bonded to the tower. High up in this wall are two narrow round-headed windows, with baluster shafts set in the wall beside them; these shafts were turned round and re-set in the last century. An effigy of a priest lies on the floor beside the pulpit. The glass cases in the north transept contain a collection of stones which belonged to the early church.

The chancel is 14th century but contains no ancient windows. The east window contains modern glass, one panel depicts Benedict Biscop superintending the building of the tower. The legless figure which lies on a panelled altar tomb under a modern canopy is thought to be the effigy of William, Lord Hylton (died 1435) who built Hylton Castle.

As one stands outside and views this building which has survived the air-raids of the last war and the raids of Danish pirates almost 1,100 years ago, one feels truly awed before such antiquity.

Norton

The village of Norton with its spacious green is about two miles from Stockton. At its north-west corner stands the church, dedicated to St Mary the Virgin. The building is most interesting, being the only surviving cruciform Saxon church in the county. The tower rises from the intersection and, together with the transepts, dates from pre-Conquest times.

The nave has north and south aisles; the arcades of both aisles are Transitional, about 1180–90. The arches are pointed and of two moulded orders. The piers are cylindrical and the capitals are carved with the volute. The arches which open from the tower into the nave and chancel are round-headed but are of the same date as those of the nave arcades. The arch between the south aisle and transept and a window in the east end of the same transept are of the above dates. The clerestory windows were re-opened in 1875, five of these are round-headed and the sixth, the centre one of the south side which was inserted in the 15th century consists of two lights, the lintel being a 13th century grave-cover.

The north and south transepts open from the tower with two arches. The north transept was formerly called the Blakiston Porch and was a chantry founded by some member of the Blakiston family. This transept retains more original features than the south one. The three-light window is of recent date. There is an early piscina in the east wall, also traces of a blocked window. There is a painting on the north wall viz. 'Recognition at Emmaus' by Caravaggio. The south transept was called the Pity Porch. The south wall has been rebuilt. A narrow window in the east wall is probably a Norman insertion.

Tower arches.

The tower has an angular headed window overlooking the roofs on each of its four sides. These windows once looked into the church. The head of each window consists of two large slabs of stone laid against each other. The lines of the ancient roofs rise above these windows. Originally the tower was no higher than these lines. Then it was lighted from without by eight small openings, two on each side. These still exist, some are formed out of a single stone. The upper part of the tower was a chamber, entry being through a doorway in its south wall reached by a ladder from the south transept. The doorway can still be seen but the floor has been removed. Beneath the tower lies a 14th century sepulchral effigy, a knight in chain armour.

Some interlaced carving of Saxon date is visible on the inner face of the south-east pier. The upper stage of the tower dates from the 15th century.

The chancel was rebuilt about the middle of the 13th century. The east window and the two in the south wall date from 1496. The priest's door (also of this date) has traces of a holy stoup on its east side. In the south wall there is a sedilia and part of another; the arch moulding of the former is of beautiful design.

The original east window had four lancets, remains of which are still in evidence. A beautiful stained glass window to Bernard Gilpin, Apostle of the North, one-time Vicar of Norton, exists on the south side of the choir stalls.

A mutilated effigy of a lady (circa 14th century) is inserted in one of the walls of the south porch.

In the churchyard are many memorials; one of the most interesting being that of John Walker (died 1859), the inventor of the friction match.

There is a fine example of Saxon 'long and short' work on the north-west corner of the north transept.

Pittington

The village of Pittington is quite near to Sherburn. The church, hidden among the trees at the south end of the village, is dedicated to St Lawrence and is of great interest. It dates from about 1083 when it was aisleless. A Saxon church existed before then. About 1180 the north aisle was added. This was done by inserting arches into the wall of the nave then removing the wall between the arches. The old round-headed Norman windows of the nave were left above the arches. During the 13th century the south aisle was added in the same manner, the builder for some reason taking down the fifth bay of the north aisle at the east end and erecting in its place an arch exactly like those of the south arcade.

About this time the tower arch was erected but the upper part of the tower itself was not added until the 14th century.

In 1846 great alterations took place. The chancel with its arch was destroyed and rebuilt; the south aisle and most of the north were rebuilt, and the nave was once again lengthened. The two eastern arches date from then.

Above the north arcade, in the splay of the westernmost of the ancient Norman windows, a fragment of mural painting represents an incident in the life of St Cuthbert.

By far the most striking feature of the church, however, is the north arcade with its columns and their raised spiral moulding which is unique in the county.

The present font is the original Norman one; its bowl was found in use as a cattle trough on a farm at Belmont.

North arcade.

A collection of early grave-covers lies in the tower basement. Two grave-covers cut on one stone and separated by a groove probably commemorate male twins – each cover bears a small sword. A grave-cover of Frosterley marble in the south aisle is to one of Bishop Pudsey's stonemasons, named Christian.

The position of the tower staircase is unusual for instead of its being in one corner it projects from the centre of the north wall. The belfry contains three bells, all pre-Reformation date and inscribed. The ancient timber framing is in the form of an inverted 'T' which is unusual.

In the wall of the north aisle is a tablet to the memory of Mary Ann Westrop who was 'murdered in 1830 at nearby Hallgarth mill', this no longer exists.

A sun dial inserted in the south wall of the nave is probably Saxon. Near to the entrance to the vestry lies the effigy of a knight in full armour – circa 1250.

The age of the clerestory is uncertain but before its insertion the building must have been very dark as the only light would come from the small Norman windows.

Redmarshall

The village of Redmarshall is one of the smallest in the county and except for the church is not of great beauty or interest, it lies about 2 miles south of Bishopton.

The church, dedicated to St Cuthbert, is Norman, and consists of chancel, nave, with a chapel on the south side, and a tower at the west end. Entrance to the church is by the south doorway of a modern porch. This doorway is of Norman work, and was moved to its present position on the erection of the porch.

The tower is Norman with the exception of the parapet, which was added in the 14th century. The tower arch is a plain high Norman arch.

The nave is fitted with oak pews with open backs which have turned balusters, these date from about 1630. The windows which are supposed to be copies of the originals, are all 19th century.

The nave opens into the chancel by a Norman arch. The chancel was rebuilt in the 13th century. In the north wall there is an arched Easter Sepulchre recess, an insertion of Perpendicular date. In the south wall there are three Perpendicular sedilia. There is a priest's doorway in this wall, and a walled up low-side window. The door is now covered by a porch, and used as the vicar's vestry.

The chantry chapel called Claxton's Porch on the south side of the nave was built in the 13th century. It opens to the nave by a wide arch, which rests on corbels of an unusual character, one is of a man and the other a woman who appears to be supporting the arch with her hands. The Chantry is lit by a lovely four-light Perpendicular window in the south wall. In this chapel are the effigies, carved from alabaster of Thomas de Langton of Wynyard and his wife Sybil. This Thomas died in 1440, and the effigies give us a good idea of the dress of the period.

The first register dated 1564, which we inspected, was in a good state of preservation.

Ryton

The village of Ryton stands on a hill in the extreme north-west corner of the county on the south bank of the Tyne.

The church, dedicated to the Holy Cross, is early 13th century, with the exceptions of one or two recent additions, and consists of chancel, nave with north and south aisles, south porch and a western tower with spire, rising to a height of 108 ft.

The nave is divided from the aisles by arcades of three pointed arches resting on two pillars. In both cases the eastern pillars are octagonal and the western ones cylindrical. The font is a large circular basin resting on a cluster of shafts. The tower rests on four pointed arches which in turn rest on moulded corbels.

The chancel is divided from the nave by a pointed arch resting on moulded corbels; the south one bears the nail-head ornament. The east window is modern. The south side was originally an arcade of six lancets. The eastern one has been widened and is now a window of two lights. A low-side window has been blocked. There is a piscina with projecting basin and a priest's doorway. Five memorial tablets fixed to the north wall relate to the Bunny family.

In the sanctuary there is a remarkable effigy of Frosterley marble. It is of a deacon; he lies with tonsured head resting on a cushion, his hands clasping a large book on which is carved a dove, and his feet resting on a lion. The wood work of the chancel is mainly 17th century work. The chancel screen and choir stalls should be noted for the carving on the bench ends.

Close to the north wall of the churchyard there is a large tumulus nearly 20 ft high covered with trees.

Sadberge

This village, about four miles north-east of Darlington, is on top of a hill in otherwise flat country and commands a lovely view of the Cleveland Hills.

The church, dedicated to St Andrew, occupies the site of the castle which once existed there. The entrance to the churchyard is by a Lych gate at the side of which are steps in the wall. From the churchyard a magnificent view is obtainable of the western and south-eastern parts of the County.

The church is a low building and consists of nave, chancel and south porch and a choir vestry at the west end. A bell-cot is on the west gable. The church is modern, 1831, but contains a few remains of the earlier building. In the east end is a memorial window to the Garmondsway family, it is probable that this family originally came from near Coxhoe where traces of a medieval village bearing this name are still visible.

In the porch a stone above the door representing 'the Fall' is all that remains of the Saxon church.

Another carved stone in the porch representing 'Our Lord trampling on Satan' and the old stoup still in Its original position are all that remain of the Norman church, about AD 1266 together with a stone high up on the south wall of the chancel.

Outside on the gable of the choir vestry can be seen the base of a Norman finial cross with a new shaft.

A pre-Reformation bell dedicated to the Virgin Mary hangs in the choir vestry.

St Andrew Auckland

St Andrew, Auckland, or South Church, is the ancient parish church of Bishop Auckland and stands about a mile from the market place. A church existed here in very early Saxon or Norman times.

The church of St Andrew is one of the largest and one of the finest in the county and was collegiate. It consists of nave with north and south aisles, chancel, transepts, south porch with a chamber above, and a western tower. The building is nearly all of one date, early 13th century. The chancel was altered by Bishop Bek towards the end of the 13th century and the south transept was added by him. Cardinal Langley added a clerestory to the nave early in the 15th century and took down the spire, adding a battlemented stage to the tower. In the late 19th century several restorations took place: the chancel arch was inserted in 1864 and the south transept was nearly all rebuilt in 1881.

The south porch, through which entrance is made into the church, and that of St Helens, Auckland, are the only ones of their kind in the county having a chamber above. The outer and inner doorways are beautiful examples of Early English work. The chamber above the porch was once used by a chantry priest and later in the 17th century was occupied by the parish clerk.

On entering the church one is immediately impressed by the arcades of the nave. These are alternatively an octagonal pier and a pier of four large and four smaller shafts. In the base of the tower are the remains of an 8th century Saxon cross, one of the most important in the county, found in 1881 during restorations.

The north transept has a two light window under a segmental arch in the north end. In the east wall there is a trefoil-headed piscina. The south transept, as already stated, was rebuilt last century and is a copy of the earlier one.

The chancel has a low-slide window in the north wall and a large square aumbry. The south wall has two piscinae placed in a recess the arch of which has been destroyed. Next to these is a single sedile and west of this again two sedilia. Originally there were three but the third was destroyed when the priest's doorway was inserted. The choir stalls of carved oak are of Perpendicular work and were presented by Cardinal Langley in 1417. Two of the misericords show his coat-of-arms.

As already stated the tower originally had a spire. The oldest part is up to the corbel table. In 1417 the highest stage was added and the spire removed. In the west wall of the lowest stage there are two original lancet windows.

In the nave close to the base of the tower there are two effigies, one being of a cross-legged knight carved in oak dated about 1330 and the other of a lady, late 14th century. Fixed to the wall there is a large brass to a priest dated about 1400.

South-west of the church is a farm called East Deanery. This was originally the prebends of the Collegiate church. The site was given by Bishop Bek in 1291. It is a very interesting group of buildings. The ground floor room has a tunnel vault. Several of the ancient windows have been blocked in.

St Helen Auckland

The village of St Helen's perhaps best known for its factories is about 3 miles south-west of Bishop Auckland.

The church, as the name of the village implies, is dedicated to St Helen and dates from the late 12th to early 13th century. It consists of nave with north and south aisles, chancel with chapels on each side, a south porch with vestry above, and a bell-cot on the west gable.

The porch dates from the 15th century and the room above is now used as a vestry (e.g. St Andrew's, Auckland). The iron studded door which leads into the church from the porch is the original Perpendicular one.

The eastern arcades of the nave aisles are of Transitional date. The western ones were probably about 20 years later. These nave aisles have been extended eastwards to embrace part of the chancel; this took place about 1233 when a chantry was founded by Robert Forester and his wife. The arches belonging to the chantries are pointed and rest on corbels at the end of each arcade. The capitals of the piers which are octagonal bear the waterleaf ornament. The clerestory windows are late Perpendicular, with the exception of the west window at the end of the south aisle which is Norman. In the south aisle can be seen steps projecting from the wall; these originally led to the upper storey above the porch which probably housed a chantry priest.

The font is a round basin resting on a cylindrical shaft and is Norman. In 1845 the south wall was taken down and rebuilt. Three skulls, one of them intact, were found in the masonry.

The roofs of both chancel and nave are of black oak and date from circa 1500.

The chancel arch is 13th century as is the chancel. In the sanctuary there is a memorial brass, half hidden, dating from about 1450. It depicts a man with his wife and a group of three daughters beneath her. Beneath the man are six sons but these are hidden by the altar steps. In the side walls of the chancel there is a two-light window of late Perpendicular date. The north chapel of the chancel was restored to Our Lady in 1951. The chancel stalls are 17th century work.

The family vault of the Eden's, ancestors of Sir Anthony Eden, stands in the churchyard in front of the east window.

The bell-cot contains two bells, one is medieval and inscribed.

Seaham

Seaham is not so well known as its neighbour Seaham Harbour founded by the third Marquis of Londonderry in 1828.

The only two objects of interest at Seaham are the church and the Hall. It was at the Hall in 1815 that Lord Byron married Anne Isabella Milbanke and their signatures can be seen in the marriage register held in the safe at the church.

The church stands on the brink of a small dene which leads to the sea. It consists of chancel, nave, western tower and south porch.

The tower is 13th century and has a lofty arch, which has been renewed, opening into the nave. The battlemented parapet was added in the 14th century beneath this there is a corbel table.

The chancel contains masonry of two different types, that in the lower part of the walls is of early Norman origin. The two windows in the east end are of late Transitional date. Some of the chancel stonework bears Roman tooling. On the west side of the massive buttress against the south wall there can be seen a hand hold often found on Roman masonry. There is a double piscina in the south wall of the chancel; at the back of one, the stone bears a carving of a priest's hand raised in blessing. The chancel arch is modern but terminates in two ancient corbels bearing human faces.

The nave is filled with old box pews and has a Jacobean pulpit. The font has a line of foliage carved around the basin and is very similar to that at Dalton-le-Dale. Beside the pulpit there is a piscina and to the right of the vestry door another. The vestry contains some herringbone masonry and there is some on the exterior north wall of the church.

Over the porch there is a sundial, dated 1773. The porch has a stone slab roof which rests on two chamfered ribs. The parapets of the nave and chancel were added in the 14th century.

Sedgefield

The town of Sedgefield lies about 9 miles north of Stockton. It is a quiet place with the church towering over the surrounding quaint old houses and village green. On the north side of the churchyard there is a row of Almshouses founded by Thos Cooper in 1703 and then rebuilt in the 19th century. The town still retains two customs which are unique in this part of the country. One is the curfew, which has been carried out since the 11th century when the church bell is rung every night. The other is the annual Shrove Tuesday football match a survival from the 13th century when the Tradesmen versus the Farmers.

The church dedicated to St Edmund the Bishop, is one of the finest in the county. It is of cruciform design, and except for the tower dates from the 13th century.

The nave has north and south aisles. The arcades of the nave are uniform in character, and consist in each case of three pointed arches. The piers consist of four clustered cylinders standing on a square plinth, and have moulded bands at mid-height. The capitals are carved with foliage, flowers, birds and human figures. The pointed arches spring from corbels of human heads and are ornamented with zig-zag and filetted mouldings. These pillars are the earliest specimens of their style in the country.

The transepts open to the aisles by pointed arches of two orders. The north transept, has in the north wall a five-light window with flowing tracery. In the east wall there is a three-light window of late Decorated date. On the ledge of west window there is the altar stone of St Catherine's chapel, which was in the north transept, built in 1379. The south transept was a chantry dedicated to St Thomas. It contains two pointed recesses in the south wall each occupied by an effigy to benefactors. One is of a male, badly mutilated, the other is of a female. In the east wall there are two piscinae, one is trefoiled headed.

In the nave the south door is of one order, and has a pointed arch. West of this door there is an original lancet now blocked. In the north wall there is a blocked pointed doorway, the label of the moulding has the nail-head ornament. The windows of the nave are modern.

The tower is Perpendicular, and is of the first half of the 15th century. It is 90 ft high and is in three stages, with big angle buttresses, ending in small octagonal turrets, surmounted by spiralets within a miniature parapet. The walls of the tower have battlemented parapets. The tower arch is of two orders and both are carried down the jambs without any break. The belfry contains five bells, one being pre-Reformation. The weight of the tower on the nave at the west end has caused the arches of both aisles to lean towards the east.

The font is of black marble and is 15th century. It is octagonal and has on each of its sides the coats-of-arms of local families, carved sometime in the 18th century.

The chancel arch is of one order, the arch dies into the side walls of the chancel. The chancel is of the same date as the north transept. The east window is of five-lights with flowing tracery of late Decorated date. Against the north wall there is a very interesting tomb. It is of Sir Andrew de Stanley the first Master of Greatham Hospital, who died in 1285. The inscription in Norman-French reads 'for the love of God pray for his soul'. The walls are panelled in black oak 8 ft high, and the stalls in the same wood have seven seats at each side. The oak chancel screen, and the woodwork mentioned, is that of Bishop Cosins time about 1660, as in Durham Cathedral.

There are several brasses in the church. The two most interesting are in the nave. One is of a lady kneeling, and by the dress, is 14th century. The other is of two skeletons in shrouds lying in coffins. There is a box pew to the left of the chancel steps.

Outside in the churchyard in the north-west corner there is a memorial to a soldier who fell in the battle of Balaklava 1854.

THIS STONE
IS
ERECTED BY
HIS FRIENDS
IN MEMORY OF
FREDERICK HARDWICKE
(BOLTON)
AGED 21 Yrs.
SERGANT
IN THE
VI TH
INISKILLIN DRAGOONS
WHO FELL IN THE
MEMORABLE CHARGE
OF
HEAVY CAVALRY
AT
BALAKLAVA
ON THE 25TH OF OCTOBER
MDCCCLIV
BELOVED BY ALL WHO KNEW HIM

Sherburn Hospital

Sherburn Hospital is about three miles east of Durham, not to be confused with the village of Sherburn. It derives its name from 'Sheerburn' or clear stream.

The hospital was founded about 1181 by Bishop Pudsey and was for the housing of 65 lepers. Nearly all the buildings were destroyed by the Scots shortly after 1300 and of these all that remains is the south wall of the church with its three round-headed lancet windows, and the battlemented gateway.

Entry into the church is by a south door in the tower. The tower has been much renewed, except on the north side which is original.

The rest of the church was entirely rebuilt in 1868. The font is modern, the basin is square resting on a large cylindrical shaft and has a slender shaft of marble at each corner.

The arcade into the north aisle consists of two wide round arches, the plinths of the piers are original. In the south wall of the chancel there are three sedilia with ogee trefoiled arches, a piscina and an aumbry. A brass plate set in the first step of the sanctuary bears the inscription:-

THOMAS LEAVER PREACHER
TO KING EDWARD THE SIXTH
HE DIED IN IVLY 1577

Thomas Leaver was master of the hospital from 1562 until his death.

In the tower there is only one bell which was cast in 1724.

The communion cup bears the London date letter 1564–65.

During the Civil wars when the King's Army was stationed at Durham and Cromwell's at Quarrington Hill, the hospital was plundered for its cattle and goods.

Sockburn

Sockburn is about seven miles south-east of Darlington, the nearest place being Neasham, a walking distance of about two and a half miles. It is situated in a peninsula and is one of the quietest places in the county.

Here we have another of the worm legends. In a field beside the Hall there is a large slab of limestone, beneath which, according to the legend, rests the remains of the worm slain by Sir John Conyers.

The church, dedicated to All Saints, is now a ruin and stands in the grounds of the Hall. It ceased to be used as a place of worship in 1838. A new church was built on the Yorkshire side of the river at Girsby as most of the parish is in Yorkshire.

The 13th century church probably stands on the site of a Saxon building as Saxon remains have been found in the churchyard. The east wall of the chancel has three lancet windows. The 13th century chancel arch is of two orders, the inner one resting on half circular corbels. The nave arcade of two pointed arches rests on a cylindrical pier. On the north side of the nave there is a restored 15th century chapel, burial place of the Conyers, now the only part of the church in its entirety. In this chapel there is a collection of pre-Conquest crosses and grave-covers. Here is the 14th century effigy of Sir John Conyers, descendant of Sir John Conyers, the slayer of the 'dreaded Sockburn worm'. He is dressed in chain mail and a surcoat; he grasps a sword with his right hand and his feet rest on a lion and dragon in conflict.

The poet Coleridge visited Sockburn in 1799 and whilst staying there had an amorous affair with Sarah Hutchinson of Sockburn Farm. Together they visited the church and the visit is perpetuated for ever in these lines:

> She leant against the armėd man
> The statue of the armėd knight!
> She stood and listened to my lay
> Amid the lingering night.

Staindrop

Staindrop, a small pleasant country town, is about six miles from Barnard Castle. In the vicinity stands the lovely castle of Raby with its spacious park and deer.

The church of St Mary the Virgin is one of the most interesting in the county and dates from pre-Conquest times. The present building is a mixture of various styles of architecture. The oldest part is the nave which has north and south arcades of very early Norman work dating from about 1170. Above the eastern arches of both arcades can be seen blocked in Saxon windows. The western bays of both arcades are of a later date than the others, approximately 1250. The roof and clerestory are both 15th century.

The tower was erected about the middle of the 13th century and is supported on pointed arches. The belfry was a 15th century addition, probably replacing a spire; it contains six bells dated 1788.

The aisles are Transitional, approximately 1170, the south being the most interesting. In the east end of the south aisle there is a lovely five-light window. The west end contains a window consisting of three sharply pointed lancets which was originally the south window in the south transept. In the south wall there is a triple sedilia and two sepulchral niches. Beside the sedilia there is a door leading into the chantry priest's porch, a peculiar stone-flagged erection on the exterior south-east corner of the south aisle. In the plain niche lies the effigy of a female and child (about 1260). In the enriched recess lies another effigy thought to represent Euphemia Clavering, mother of Ralph Neville, the victorious leader at the battle of Neville's Cross (1346).

The north aisle is about the same date as the south but it is much inferior. There is a very small transept at the east end. The only lights left in the transept are the north ones, three separate lancets. In the east wall there are two piscinae showing this transept was built to receive two altars.

The chancel arch is pointed and is of two chamfered orders. There is a lovely triple sedilia, the finest example in the county, in the chancel of 15th century date. The chancel screen is the only pre-Reformation one left in the county.

At the west end of the church there is a remarkable collection of effigies. On the left as one enters by the south doorway, there is an oak monument to Henry, Vth Earl of Westmorland, who died in 1564, with, on either side of him, his first two wives, Anne and Jane. Next to this there is a mutilated effigy of a female, probably one of the Nevilles, resting on four lions. To the right of this there is a magnificent alabaster tomb to Lord Ralph Neville, 1st Earl of Westmorland, who died in 1426, and his two wives. In the west end of the north aisle there is a lovely white marble tomb to William Henry Vane, 1st Duke of Cleveland, who died in 1842.

Stanhope

The market town of Stanhope stands amidst some of the county's wildest country about fifteen miles west of Bishop Auckland.

The church, dedicated to St Thomas the Apostle, is Early English with the exception of the lower part of the tower. It consists of nave with north and south aisles, chancel with chapel on the north side, western tower and south porch. The south arcade dates from the early part of the 13th century and the north arcade slightly later. As the piers of the arcades are unusually short the level of the floor has been lowered.

The chancel arch is pointed and has corbels bearing carvings of human faces. The chancel had numerous alterations made to it in the 14th century, one being the insertion of the east window. Several of the stall ends are 17th century. On the north wall of the chancel there are two beautifully carved oak plaques representing Adam and Eve and Christ and St Peter, together with a lovely little painting of Christ and St Veronica (late 16th century).

The chapel on the north side of the chancel opens to the chancel by a segmental arch and to the north aisle of the nave by a pointed arch. This chapel was probably built in the 14th century.

The lower part of the tower is late 12th century. The glass from the 14th century window in the west wall came from the ancient chancel window and dates from the 14th and 16th centuries; the earliest fragment, the largest, shows a Bishop with mitre and crozier. The upper stage of the tower is Early English. The parapet was added in the 15th century.

Stockton

The town of Stockton has a number of distinctions. It was here the first friction match was invented by John Walker, in 1827. The first passenger railway (the Stockton and Darlington Railway) in the world operated from here. In 1825 the first passenger in the world was booked there. The High Street is said to be the widest in England, at its widest point 180 ft.

The Parish Church dedicated to St Thomas is the only church in the county designed by Sir Christopher Wren. The present building opened in 1712, stands near the site of an earlier church, a Chapel-of-Ease to Norton built in 1235.

The church contains much beautiful woodwork. The carved pew heads are of surpassing beauty and in most cases are memorials. The pulpit is the remains of the old three decker pulpit which was the last in the county.

On the west wall of the nave there is a window of special interest, this was originally the east window, and was found during restorations behind the galleries, which existed up to 1946.

The present chancel was rebuilt in 1906. The floor is formed of Frosterley, Sicilian, and Italian marbles. The Communion rails and the altar are made from oak taken from Captain Cook's ship the *Endeavour* whilst it was being repaired, before he made his last voyage round the world.

On the nave pillars there are brass memorial tablets, commemorating prominent people who lived in the neighbourhood to mention a few, Captain Cook, George Stephenson, John Walker, and Sheraton.

The tower contains ten bells, and fractures which have appeared in the walls through being 'over-belled' have caused grave concern. An appeal was launched, and work has been undertaken to remedy this fault.

Pew end.

Stranton

The village of Stranton derives its name from 'town on the strand'. It lies about a quarter of a mile from the sea and is now incorporated in the town of West Hartlepool which has grown around the old village.

The church probably occupies the site of that given by Robert de Bruce to Guisborough Abbey. Dedicated to All Saints, it consists of chancel with north aisle, nave with north and south aisles, western tower and a south porch through which entrance is made into the church.

The nave is divided from the south aisle by two equally wide arches (14th century) of two chamfered orders supported by a large octagonal pier without capitals. The arches of the north aisle are 19th century and similar in design except for a moulded octagonal capital to the pier. Part of a beautiful decorated canopy is inserted above a piscina near the east end of the south aisle. The clerestory windows in the nave have been restored at some time.

The chancel has a north aisle which was added during the

Perpendicular period. It is divided from the chancel by two wide-pointed arches resting on an octagonal pier and semi-octagonal responds with moulded capitals of the same form. In the north wall of this aisle there are two Perpendicular windows, each has two cinquefoil-headed lights. In the south wall of the chancel there is a beautiful three light window – Decorated. There is a fine piscina in the same wall, the arch of the niche is round-headed and the moulding has the square flower ornament, the basin projects.

The lower stage of the tower is Early English. It has pointed arches. The belfry has two light windows of Decorated date on each side and contains three bells, all are inscribed, one is pre-Reformation. The parapet is embattled, with gargoyles on the north and south sides. There are crocketted pinnacles at the angles and diagonal buttresses (a rare feature in the county).

Entrance to the church was originally through an archway in the north porch. This porch is now used as a choir vestry and the arch has been blocked. The south porch, of Decorated date, has stone side benches. The vestry is of the same period. A modern organ chamber has been added onto the south side of the chancel. The twolight window (Decorated) at its east end was originally in the south wall of the chancel. Fragments of ancient grave-covers are built into the west wall of this chamber.

St Oswald Durham

The church stands on the edge of the steep wooded bank of the river Wear, at thc top of Church Street.

The architecture is of various periods. The tower is of Perpendicular date and is perhaps the most interesting part of the building. To reach the first floor one climbs a very unusual stone stairway. It is composed of twenty medieval gravestones, some still bearing the symbols showing the sex and the occupation of the person they originally covered.

About the end of the 12th century the north and south aisles were added, each opening into the nave by an arcade of four semi-circular arches resting on cylindrical piers. These are beautiful examples of the Norman period during its transition. At this time a new chancel arch was built, wide and pointed, and springing from circular piers and capitals with waterleaf ornamentation.

The clerestory windows are modern and replace those of the 15th century. All that remains of the beautiful hammer beam roof of that time are the grotesque heads, and the angles bearing blank shields at the bottom of the pendant posts. The oak stall work in the chancel is 15th century. In the north aisle there is an old oak vestment chest secured by two locks.

The western window in the lower stage of the tower is a copy of the original, and depicts in stained glass the death of St Oswald.

In the 14th century the aisles were rebuilt and continued westward the length of the nave. Two new arches were added to the west end of each arcade, these have octagonal piers.

Outside the church over the south door there is a beautiful decorated niche, intended for a figure of the patron saint. The churchyard contains many interesting gravestones.

In the new burial ground across the road from the church, one can see the grave of Dr John Bacchus Dykes vicar of St Oswald's 1862–76. He is perhaps the greatest hymn writer the Church of England has known.

Processional cross c.1500.

Tanfield

Tanfield, a tiny village in the north-west part of the county, is about three miles from Stanley.

The church, dedicated to St Margaret, goes back to Norman days. The present church was rebuilt and enlarged in 1749, a sundial giving this information is let into the wall on the nave's south aisle. The tower was added in 1854 and it is through a door in its south wall that one enters into the church.

There are several memorials to the Eden and Shafto families in the nave. The chancel contains several memorials in the floor. In the south wall there is a tombstone to Sir William Wray who died in 1628. In the north wall there is a piscina decorated with the nail-head ornament, the oldest remaining part of the earlier church.

Near the village is a remarkable bridge named the Causey Arch. It has a span of 105 ft and is 80 ft high. It was built in 1727 to carry a double railway track for the transport of coal from Tanfield to Newcastle. The architect was a local stone mason Ralph Wood, who committed suicide because of his fear that the stone bridge would collapse as a wooden one he had constructed previously over the same spot had done.

The Hall a little to the south-east of the church has the finest 18th century iron gates in the county.

Trimdon

The village of Trimdon goes back to ancient times. Here King Canute alighted from his horse, and having his head shaved, travelled barefoot and bareheaded via Garmondsway to Durham Cathedral, to the shrine of St Cuthbert. Trimdon (the place of Tonsure) is supposed to have derived its name from this incident, at least it makes a nice story.

The church stands in the middle of the village, and is dedicated to St Mary Magdalene. It consists of nave with a north aisle, chancel, and a south porch. A bell-cot is on the west gable.

Entrance is by the south porch, the doorway is a plain pointed arch of one order. The south and west walls of the nave, the south and east walls, and part of the north wall of the chancel are ancient.

The chancel arch is Norman and is greatly depressed owing to the shrinking of the side walls. It is of two orders, the centre one is square, and the inner one chamfered.

The most remarkable feature in the church is a 'low side window' occupying a position in the south wall of the chancel, and believed to be the earliest example of such in the county. There is a rebate for a window shutter on the exterior face.

The church was probably built about 1100, and the north aisle was added in 1873.

The churchyard is very small, and a new burial ground stands at the east end of the village. Here is a memorial identical with one at Kelloe to the Trimdon Grange Colliery disaster in 1882.

Washington

The village of Washington lies about 4 miles from Boldon, and 6 miles from Sundcrland.

The church, dedicated to St Mary the Virgin, was built in 1831 and occupies the site of an earlier church.

Entry into the church is by a porch at the west end. The door leading into the church from the porch is where the west window of the old church was situated. This gives some idea of how much higher the present building is from the old one.

Inside to the right of this door stands the font which is of Frosterley marble and dates from the 12th century. Above the font on the wall hangs a picture of George Washington, with the flag of the USA above. There is a gallery in the church which was erected for the children of the parish. The windows in the nave are all long lancets, those on the north side contain modern stained glass representing scenes from the life of Our Lord.

The walls of the sanctuary are painted with the motif I.H.S. The organ case and pipes are beautifully painted. The choir stalls are of plain oak with shields of various families carved and painted on them. The east window is a memorial to the men of the village who fell in the 1914–18 war. It contains in the left and right lights portraits of famous people in English history who have died in the faith of Jesus Christ. The ceiling of the church is of an unusual design.

The village claims fame in having produced the ancestors of George Washington. Close to the church on the south side is the Hall, the ancestral home of the Washingtons. It is of Jacobean date, and has recently been restored.

The arms and crest of the family were chosen as the emblems of the USA in honour to the first President viz. Stars on the flag. Eagle on the Standard.

Whickham

Whickham lies about 4 miles west of Gateshead and stands on high land overlooking the broad valley of the lower Tyne.

The church, dedicated to St Mary the Virgin, stands above an open space aptly called Church Green. It was restored in 1862 but still retains three styles of architecture.

The present building consists of a chancel, nave with a south aisle, and two north aisles, a south porch, and a western tower.

Entry into the church is through the south porch, which has in its west wall two medieval grave-covers, each bearing a carved cross. Above the outside doorway there is a sundial dated 1651.

The nave is unusual in having two modern north aisles. The south arcade is of Transitional date, and is very late 12th century and consists of four bays. The arches are round and rest on cylindrical piers. The capitals of these piers are unusual they have square abaci with waterleaf ornamentation.

The font is round and carved from Frosterley marble. The windows are modern, and in some cases are reproductions and contain some fine coloured glass.

The chancel arch is the oldest part of the church, it is late Norman. It consists of two square orders resting on cushioned capitals. The north one is carved with a flower ornament.

The priest's door in the south wall of the chancel is probably Norman, or Transitional. The sanctuary contains two 17th century armchairs.

The tower is of Early English date except for the parapet which was added in the 15th century. The lower stage is a pointed stone vault. The higher stage has a two light belfry window on each side. The bells are modern.

Whitburn

Whitburn is one of the most beautiful villages in the county, but is probably not so well known by the visitor to the seaside as nearby Seaburn.

The church consists of nave, chancel, north and south aisles, a tower, and a south porch. The church dates back to the 13th century with the exception of the upper part of the tower. This was added in the 15th century and is surmounted by a short spire.

On the south wall of the tower is a sundial. The belfry contains two bells, both of pre-Reformation date. Built into the outside wall of the south aisle is an inscribed medieval grave-cover. At the west end of the south aisle there are two more. The churchyard contains many ancient memorials, and a stone coffin minus the lid rests beside the porch.

Inside, the church has rather an austere appearance. The east window is modern. There are four lancets in the south wall, and one in the north wall of the chancel, all of which are restored. A low-side window is in the usual position, but from the inside this is blocked by a seat in the choir stalls.

The nave is divided from the aisles by arcades. There are five arches to each, which are pointed and of two chamfered orders. With the exception of a vesica-piscis light in the west end of the south aisle, the nave contains no ancient windows. The arch opening into the tower from the nave is of three orders, of which the two inner ones are ancient.

There is a memorial plaque in the south aisle to a Lieutenant in the Scots Greys who died of wounds the 26th August 1900, and was buried at Pretoria, Transvaal, South Africa.

In the north aisle there is a memorial window to one Thomas Wilson Ranson of Sunderland who died at sea the 2nd June 1871.

In the west end of the south aisle there is an effigy to Michael Matthew of Cleadon, who died in 1689. The figure holds an open book in the right hand, with the text inscribed on it 'I shall not lye here, but rise'. This effigy is very unusual and gives the visitor an opportunity for a study of the dress of the late 17th century.

One can hardly realize, in this typical country churchyard, just how near the sea is, except for an occasional moan of a ship's hooter.

Whitworth

The village of Whitworth is about two miles distance from Spennymoor, and it is a very pleasant walk from the one to the other, each side of the road being bordered by neat clipped hedges.

The church itself stands quite near to Whitworth Hall, onetime home of 'Bobby Shafto' of the famous song.

It consists of chancel and nave, with a south porch. On the west gable there is a bell-cot containing one bell, this was cast in 1850 from two bells and inscribed R. SHAFTO. 1727. The present church was entirely rebuilt in 1850. The original church which was Norman, was founded in 1183, and was served by the monks of nearby Merrington. The first curate was in 1427.

Under the west gable-end are two sepulchral effigies placed there in 1935. One is of great interest, being a knight in full armour. On the head is a cylindrical helmet, the apertures for the sight and the weldings or joints forming a cross. The legs are crossed and trample on a human figure, at the right side is a couchant hound. The effigy is in a state of defence the shield borne before the body, the sword half drawn from its sheath. This is probably the effigy of Thomas de Acle who died in 1290. The female effigy is badly mutilated, the head is missing. The hands are folded in the act of prayer. The body is in a loose gown, and a cloak or mantle hangs from the shoulders. This effigy dates from the 13th century and is probably the wife of the above knight.

It is to be pitied that these effigies, although protected by a roof, are still somewhat exposed to the elements.

Winston

The village of Winston stands on a hill overlooking the river Tees. The most outstanding feature of the place is the stone bridge, which has one arch with a span of 112 ft. From the churchyard there is a magnificent view, with the sound of the river rushing over its rock strewn bed, through the lovely wooded valley. We can here fully appreciate the wonderful bridge and admire its lofty span.

The church is dedicated to St Andrew and consists of chancel, nave with a south aisle, and a south porch, an octagonal bell-tower with spire attached a 19th century addition.

The nave is divided from the south aisle by an arcade of three pointed arches. Only the two eastern ones are ancient, and these are of 13th century date. They rest on a cylindrical pier which has a round moulded capital and an octagonal base. The font is 13th century; on the bowl are carved dragons in conflict, also foliage and patterns of window tracery. On the floor beside the font lies a 13th century floriated grave-cover, on the floral cross are perched birds.

The chancel has a beautiful eastern window of three lancets these are the originals. In the south wall there is a piscina, which has a line of nutmeg ornament round the chamfer. There are several 17th century bench-ends in the choir stalls.

Witton Gilbert

The village is situated in a valley about four miles north-west of Durham and on the south overlooks the valley of the river Browney. Witton Gilbert is first mentioned in the latter half of the 12th century when Gilbert de la Ley was Lord of the Manor at Witton. It was this Gilbert who founded and endowed the hospital for lepers dedicated to St Mary Magdalene, and now part of Witton Hall Farm. The farm is close to the church on the north side. A walled-in 13th century window of two Pointed lights, with ornamented mouldings is the only feature of interest remaining.

The church is dedicated to St Michael and All Angels, and stands on a knoll to the south of the village. Entrance to the churchyard is by a lychgate erected in 1905, and to the church by a porch at the west end. There is a nave with a north aisle, and a chancel.

The church dates from the 12th century and was originally one of the four chapels-of-ease in the parish of St Oswald's of Durham. The only remains of the early church are two small round-headed windows in the south wall. A doorway in the south wall is now walled up. The north doorway was removed during restorations in the 19th century and inserted at the west end. The base of the font probably dates from the 12th century. There is a piscina in the south wall of the chancel, which is of the same date.

In the 14th century the church was restored. The east window, consisting of three lights under a pointed arch, belongs to this time. A square-headed window of two lights is found at the east end of the south wall in the nave. This contains fragments of 14th century glass, found in windows of the north wall, and inserted here in the 19th century when restorations took place.

A gallery which was erected at the west end in 1742 was removed in the 19th century restorations. The present windows except those already mentioned were inserted. The altar rails, and the reading desk were made from the wood of the old rafters of the roof. The painted glass in the east window was inserted at this time, also two pieces of ancient glass were incorporated in the tracery.

Outside the church, built into the west wall, above the window at the end of the north aisle, is a sculptured stone of early date. It shows a hand in the act of blessing. In the bell-cot over the west gable there are two bells, which were recast in 1948 and bear the inscription C.H. M.E. FECIT. A.D. MDCXCIII.

Witton-le-Wear

The village of Witton-le-Wear is about four miles from Bishop Auckland, situated on a hill round which the river Wear sweeps on its south, east and west sides. A fine view of Witton Castle is obtained from the village street. The surrounding country is charming, and the air very invigorating.

The church which was rebuilt in 1902 occupies the site of an early Norman church. It consists of nave with north aisle, and a chancel, a bell turret is on the west gable.

The main entrance into the church is by the south porch. The aisle is divided from the nave by an arcade of three pointed arches, resting on round pillars. These have been rebuilt and are the only remaining ancient parts of the earlier church.

The chancel is very tastefully decorated, the walls and ceiling are painted. On the north wall of the chancel there is a 17th century helmet, and above it the mutilated stone figure of an animal, both were found in the neighbourhood. Within the altar rails stands a 17th century carved chair.

The shaft of an ancient cross now supporting a sundial, stands in the churchyard on the south side.

Wolsingham

The town of Wolsingham is ten miles north-west of Bishop Auckland. Along the road which leaves the town for Stanhope there are several 17th century houses.

The church is off the main thoroughfare at the end of a small side street, and makes a pleasing picture with its yew lined path leading to the south porch.

Dedicated to St Mary and St Stephen the church consists of a chancel, nave with side aisles, a south porch and western tower. The church was rebuilt in 1848 except for the lower part of the tower which is of Transitional date.

The modern pointed tower arch which opens to the nave rests on ancient corbels carved with grotesque heads. In the base of the tower there is a grave-cover fixed to the wall. The baptistry at the west end of the south aisle was opened up in 1896. In its west stained glass window is depicted Jacob's dream.

The north aisle has a memorial at the west end to a local schoolmaster and curate who died in 1821. Within the altar rails there are two old armchairs of carved oak.

Outside high up on the west wall of the tower just below the windows of the belfry there is a blocked in round-headed window, the only remaining window of the early church.

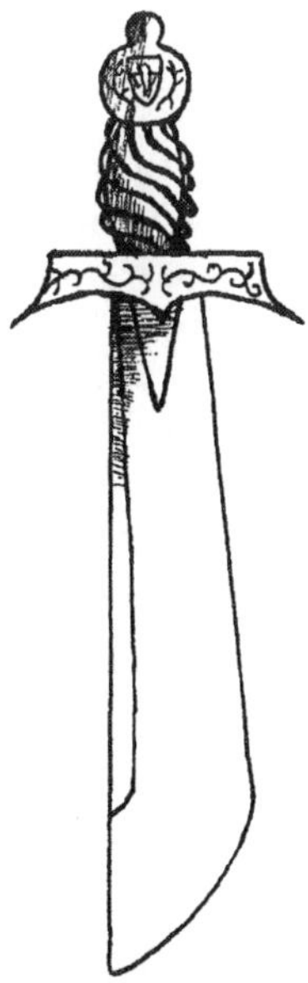

Conyers faulchion.

Periods of Architecture

AD 600–1066

Pre-Conquest or Saxon

This is distinguished by rough walls with 'long-and-short' work at the corners, flat pilasters, and string-courses. Doorways are circular-headed or triangular. Windows are circular-headed, or triangular and splayed outside and in, belfries often have two lights with a baluster between. Arches and jambs have stones the width of the wall and are intercepted by imposts. The chief ornaments are roll-moulding, knot- and plait-work and crude figures. Saxon work is often very crude. Examples: Escomb, Hart, Jarrow, Monkwearmouth, Norton, Billingham. Fragments of Saxon crosses are found in several churches.

Window, south wall, Jarrow.

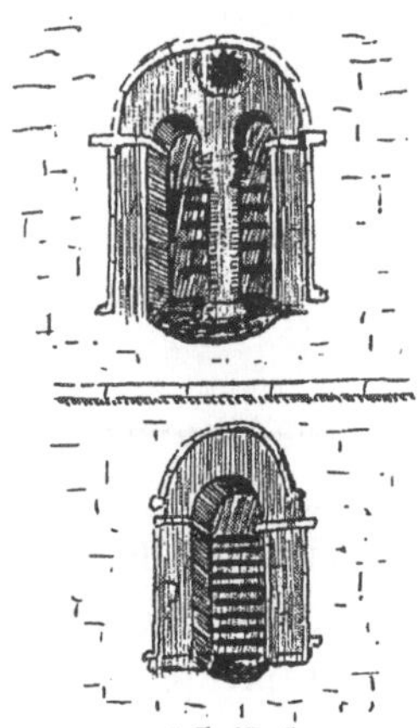

Billingham church. Saxon windows in tower.

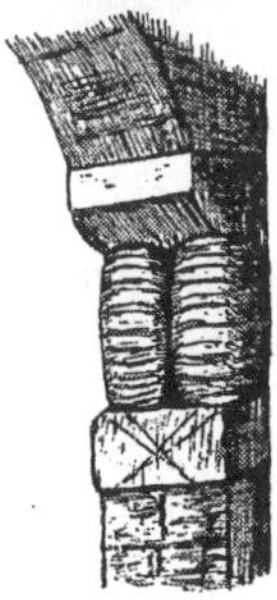

Saxon balaster shafts in porch doorway of Monkwearmouth church.

Doorway, Jarrow monastery.

Norman 1066–1200

Very early Norman work in which Saxon influence is still felt is often called the Saxon 'over-lap' period. Norman walls are thick, but filled with rubble and mortar. 'Herringbone' masonry is usually early Norman, though it is occasionally found in Saxon walls. Buttresses are shallow and flat, and corbel-tables appear. All arches are circular, the windows deeply recessed inside, the doors often recessed and carved. The circular piers have cushion, scallop, or volute capitals, and low bases. Early work is plain, but later there is rich ornamentation which includes zig-zag or chevron, beak-head, lozenge, medallion, roll, pellet, and figures and animals. Examples: Ebchester, Elton, Heighington, Pittington, Redmarshall, St Helen Auckland.

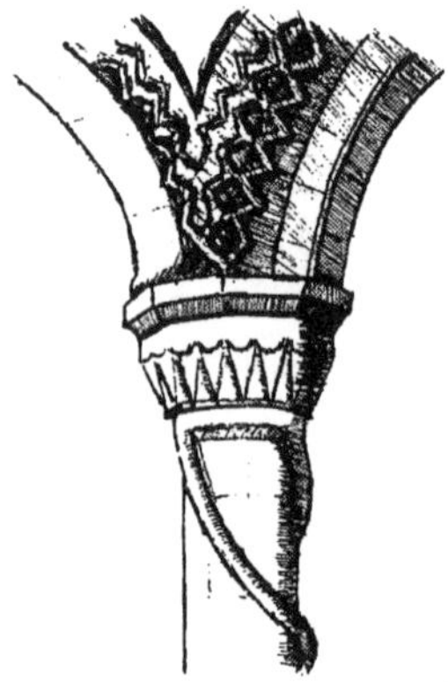

Capital, Pittington c.1175.

Transitional

The end of the Norman and the beginning of the Early English period is known as Transitional. During this time the circular Norman work was changing to the pointed Gothic, and there is a mixture of the two styles, arches being sometimes rounded and sometimes pointed. The capitals have waterleaf design, shafts are keel shaped. The chief ornamentation is the 'nutmeg'. Examples: Croxdale, Elwick Hall, Lanchester, St Helen Auckland, St Oswald Durham, Whickham.

Croxdale church, Norman doorway about 1120 A.D.

Early English 1200–1300

This marks the beginning of Gothic architecture. Walls are becoming thinner, and the slender buttresses project more. Windows, called lancets, are very narrow and pointed and are still recessed in the interior; later ones have plate-tracery. Doorways and arches are tall and pointed. Capitals are bell-shaped, and early ones have plain mouldings, and later ones stiff foliage. Piers are circular, octagonal, or have four- or eight-clustered shafts, and have 'hold-water' bases. The chief ornaments are 'nail-head', 'dog-tooth', and deeply cut mouldings. Examples: Dalton, Darlington, Easington, Gainford, Houghton-le-Spring, Hartlepool, Lanchester, Medomsley, Sedgefield.

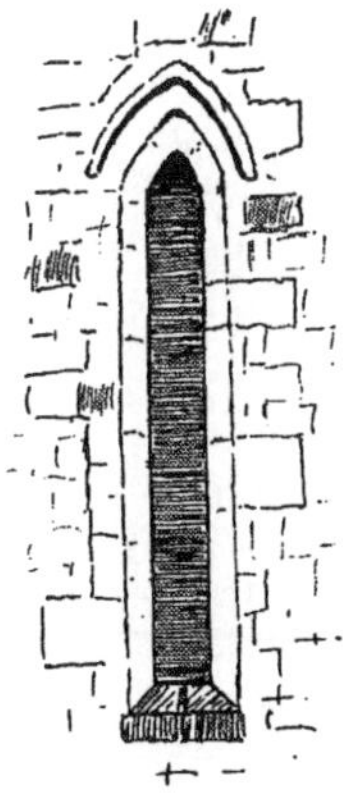

Lancet window, Dalton-le-Dale.

Capital, Sedgefield.

Decorated 1300–1400

This period is explained by its name. Buttresses are broader at the base, and the tops are often ornamented with crocketted pinnacles. Windows are wider and generally have elaborate tracery – Geometric, Reticulated, or Curvilinear – and are usually pointed, but occasionally square-headed. Arches are becoming lower, and the capitals are moulded or have natural foliage. Piers are octagonal, circular, or have shafts joined to a central mass, and the bases are higher. Doors, tombs, and niches have elaborate canopies. The chief ornaments are crockets, 'ball-flower' and 'four-petalled flower'. Examples: Brancepeth, Easington, Houghton-le-Spring, Sedgefield, Staindrop.

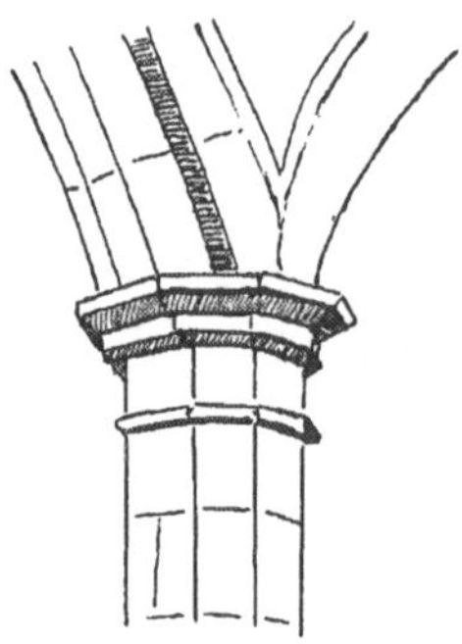

Capital, St Oswald's.

Window, Brancepeth.

Perpendicular 1400–1500

This period began with the end of the Black Death which had temporarily arrested church building. Many towers were rebuilt at this time or a stage added to the existing one; windows were inserted in older walls. Walls are battlemented, and buttresses are more massive, to take the strain of the larger windows, made to display stained glass. The windows have mullions carried to top, and the tracery is characterized by straight lines. Arches are flatter, and the piers, circular or octagonal, have tall bases. Panelling and the Tudor rose are used for ornament, and much beautiful screen work belongs to this period. Examples: Brancepeth, Chester-le-Street, Egglescliffe, Norton, Seaham, Staindrop, Stranton.

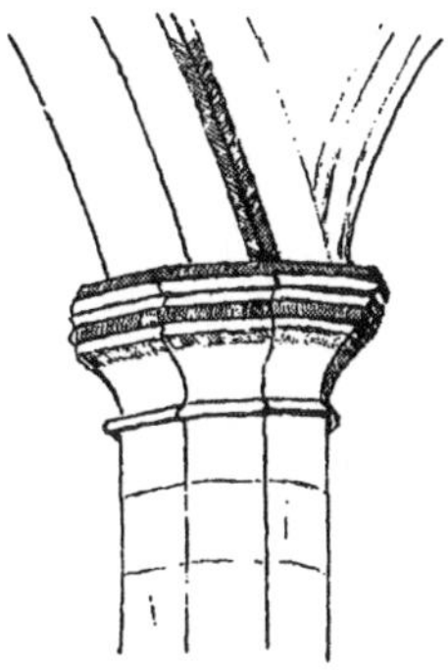

Capital, Stranton.

Window, Norton.

A

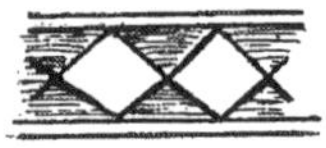
B

C

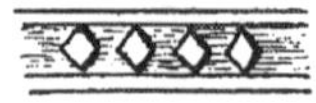
D

E

F

G

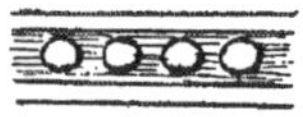
H

I

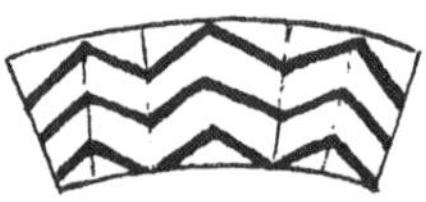
J

K

L

M

N

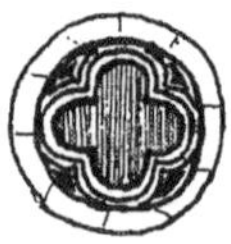
O

P

Q

R

S

T

U

V

W

X

Glossary

Abacus	The flat stone at the top of the capital of a pier.
Altar tomb	Resembling an altar.
Anchorage	Room for the housing of a recluse, or hermit.
Arcade	Range of arches supported on piers or columns.
Aumbry	Cupboard in the wall to hold sacred vessels.
Baluster	Small pillar or column of fanciful outline.
Barrel vault	Vault of semi-circular or pointed section.
Battlemented	Parapet with indentations or embrasures with a raised portion between. (Fig. S)
Bays	Compartments, each divided from the other not by walls, but by piers or columns.
Beak-heads	Row of bird or animal heads with beaks pointing down, biting onto a roll moulding. (Fig. I)
Bell-cot	Turret, usually west end, to house the bells.
Benitura	See Holy Stoup.
Billet	Ornamentation made up of short raised rectangles placed at regular intervals. (Fig. C)
Bosses	Projecting ornaments at intersecting points, generally the beams of a roof. (Fig. K)
Buttress	Mass of masonry built against a wall to give additional strength.
Capital	Head of a column.
Chantry	Chapel endowed for the saying of Masses for the soul of the founder.

Chamfer Surface made by cutting across a block of stone or wood at an angle 45°.

Chevron Sculptured moulding forming zig-zag pattern.

Cinquefoil Five leaf shapes. (Fig. P)

Clerestory The upper storey of a church, pierced with windows.

Coped grave-cover Tombstone in the shape of a house roof.

Corbel Bracket projecting from a wall to support a parapet, the beams of a roof, or an arch. (Fig. V)

Corbel table Series of corbels. (Fig. E)

Crocketted Decorations on pinnacles usually in leaf shapes. (Fig. M)

Cruciform In the shape of a cross.

Cushioned capitals Cut from a cube by having the lower angles rounded off. (Fig. F)

Cusp The small pointed member between two loves of a trefoil, quatrefoil etc. (Fig. Q)

Dogtooth Ornament consisting of four cornered stars placed diagonally and raised. (Fig. A)

Dormer Window placed vertically in the sloping plane of a roof.

Effigy Sculptured figure in stone or wood over a tomb.

Escutcheons Shield for armorial bearings. (Fig. X)

Fillet Narrow flat band running down a shaft or along a roll moulding.

Finial The termination of a pinnacle. (Fig. L)

Floriated Decorated with floral ornament.

Frosterley marble A black limestone containing fossils, quarried at Frosterley.

Gargoyle Water spout projecting from a parapet, carved in an animal or human shape. (Fig. R)

Hagioscope An opening cut in the wall, often in the chancel arch, to give a view of the altar.

Hammer beam roof Beams project at right angles from the top of a wall, to carry arched braces or struts.

Herringbone Masonry laid diagonally, forming zig-zag pattern.

Hog backed Tombstone in the shape of a low house with an arched roof, generally carved, with heads at each end.

Hood moulding Projecting moulding above arch, or lintel to throw off water.

Impost The horizontal stone on which an arch rests.

Incised Cut into or carved.

Indented Chiselled out shape.

Jambs Straight side of an archway, door, window.

Keel-shaped Outline the shape of a ship's keel.

Lancet A tall narrow window.

Light Window opening.

Linen pattern Representing a piece of linen laid in folds. (Fig. T)

Lintel Horizontal beam or stone bridging an opening.

Long and short work Quoins consisting of stones placed with the long sides alternately upright and horizontal.

Low-side window Near the ground, use is doubtful, probably for the use of lepers.

Lozenge Diamond shape. (Fig. B)

Mausoleum Family burial vault, with a domed structure built over it.

Misericord	Hinged choir stall seat with bracket underneath; when turned up provides support for the occupier during long periods of standing.
Monolithic	Cut from a single stone.
Nail-head	Ornamental motif, small pyramids regularly repeated. (Fig. D)
Niche	Small recess.
Newel	Circular or winding stairway which has a central post.
Nutmeg	Ornamental motif. (Fig. H)
Ogee	Two curves each drawn from one centre, and meeting in a point at the top.
Orders	Doorways and windows, with concentric steps receding towards the opening.
Oriel	Curved projection on an upper floor, usually a window.
Parapet	A low wall placed to protect any spot where there is a sudden drop.
Pendant post	Elongated so that it seems to hang down.
Piers	Solid support e.g. as for an arch.
Pinnacle	An ornamental conical shape, crowning a tower, spire, buttress, etc. (Fig. W)
Piscina	Stone wall basin to carry away water after washing sacred vessels.
Plinth	Projecting base of a wall or column.
Popinjay	Parrakeet or parrot.
Poppy head	An ornamental top to a bench-end, often a figure. (Fig. U)
Principal	Rafter usually corresponding to the main bay division of the nave and chancel below.

Putto	A small naked boy.
Quadripartite	One wherein one bay of vaulting is divided into four parts.
Quatrefoil	Four leaf shapes. (Fig. O)
Quoin	An external angle of a building.
Reredos	Structure behind and above the altar.
Responds	A half pier attached to the wall to support an arch.
Rood loft	Singing gallery over the rood screen.
Rood screen	A screen separating the chancel from the nave, usually supporting a large cross.
Roll moulding	Cylindrical shaped moulding.
Sedilia	Stone seat in the sanctuary for the use of the priest (usually three).
Segmental	In the form of a segment, pointed, four-centred.
Soffit	The lower surface of an arch.
Springer	Where the arch rises from its supports.
Stoup	A basin for Holy Water.
String course	Narrow horizontal moulding running round a wall.
Sanctus bell-cot	Where the Angelus would be rung from in pre-Reformation days.
Transept	Transverse portion of a church in the cruciform plan.
Trefoil	Three leaf shapes. (Fig. N)
Tympanum	Semi-circular or triangular space between the lintel and the arch of a doorway.
Tunnel vault	See Barrel vault.
Vaulting	An arched roof usually of stone.
Vesica	A pointed oval opening.

Volute A spiral scroll.

Voussoirs Wedge-shaped stones used in arches.

Water leaf Leaf shape ornamentation used on capitals. (Fig. G)

Zig-zag See Chevron. (Fig. J)

Bibliography

J.R. Boyle *Guide to Durham*, 2 vols. (1892).
Arthur Mee *The King's England, Durham.*
Nikolaus Pevsner *Buildings of England, County Durham* (1953).
Robert Surtees *The History & Antiquities of the County Palatine of Durham* 4 vols. (1816–40).
Church pamphlets.